THE
Polished
WOMAN

THE

Polished
WOMAN

Hints, Tips, and Tricks to
Getting Organized

ANGIE MASSENGILL

Library of Congress Control Number: 2010908918
ISBN: Hardcover   978-1-4535-2000-0
               Softcover   978-1-4535-1999-8
               Ebook   978-1-4535-2001-7

This book was printed in the United States of America.

To order additional copies of this book, contact:
Xlibris Corporation
1-888-795-4274
www.Xlibris.com
Orders@Xlibris.com
80249

Contents

Acknowledgments 13

Dedication 15

Life Is Short 17

Introduction 19

Rules to Live By 21

Too Many Projects...22

Get Organized...23

Working Together 24

Tools to Make Life Easier...24

Getting Started..24

Plan 25

Starting Point 25

To be Organized is a Lifestyle Change 29

Get into a Routine...30

What Stays and What Goes 30

Storage Room..32

The Outside of Your Home Is as Important as the Inside 33

No Place Like Home 34

Hints, Tips, and Tricks...34

Address Labels 34

Aging Parents 35

Air Conditioner Filters...36

Air Mattress 36

Antiques 36

Attic Storage..37

Baby Food Jars 37

Backpacks..37

Backyard Barbecues 37
Bar...38
Baskets..40
Bed Rest 40
Beverages 41
Binders 41
Birthday Cards 41
Blankets...42
Books..42
Boots 42
Broom 43
Building a New House 43
Business Cards 44
Buttons 45
Cards and Letters...45
Carpets 45
CDs..46
Ceiling Fan Blades 46
Ceiling Fans..46
Cell Phones 46
Certificate of Authenticity 48
Chest of Drawers 48
Cleaning Supplies 48
Clear Containers 48
Clothes 49
Clothing for Emergencies 49
Clothes You no Longer Wear 50
Closets..51
Clutter within Clutter...51
Coats..52
Cookbook 52
Cold Days and Nights 53
Colored Hangers...53
Cords 53

Cosmetics on a Hot Day...53
Cosmetics 54
Crystal 54
Crystal Chandelier 54
Curling Iron 55
Decorative Storage Units 55
Decorating Styles 55
Direct Deposit 56
Digital Picture Frames...56
Doctor 57
Documents 57
Dog and Cat Food 58
Dresser Drawers 58
DVDs 59
Earrings..59
Entryway..59
Emergency Contact List 60
Emergency Grab-and-Go File 61
Emergency Kit for the Home..62
Emergency Roadside Kit..62
Emergency Kit for Storm Shelter or Basememt 63
Errands...64
Fanny Pack..65
Flea Markets..65
Fireplace..67
Fireplace Odor 67
Filing System 67
Flower Vases 69
For the Less Fortunate 69
Fresh Cut Flowers..70
Frequently Called Numbers 70
Funeral 70
Gardening Tools..70
Gifts...71

Gifts for Unexpected Guest 71
Gift Bags/Boxes and Ribbons..72
Gift-wrapping Paper..72
Gift Tags 72
Girls' Night Out 73
Grease Catcher 73
Grocery List...73
Grocery Receipts 74
Guest Room 74
Handbags 75
Hats and Gloves 75
Hedges 76
His and Her Storage Space...77
Holiday Preparation..77
Holiday Shopping 78
Homemade Cleaners 79
Home Movies 81
Homework..81
Hosiery 82
Hotlines..82
Household Chores 84
Ice...85
Ice-cream Scoop 85
Iron Skillet 86
Jeans/Clothes...86
Jewelry..86
Jewelry Cleaner 86
Junk Mail...87
Karaoke Disc 88
Keepsake Items 88
Kids' Stuff..88
Kitty Litter...89
Keys 89
Keyholes 90

Kitchen Cabinets 91
Kitchen Cabinet Knobs 91
Kitchen Drawers 91
Kitchen Sink 92
Laundry 92
Laundry Room 93
Leather 93
Letters and Documents 93
Life Story 94
Lightbulbs 94
Lingo 94
Loose Change 96
Lotion 96
Magazines 96
Magnets 97
Mail 97
Mascara 98
Making the Most of Your Food Dollar 98
Meat 99
Medicine 100
Medical History 100
Message Board 101
Memory Clutter 101
Muffin Pans 102
Nails 102
Name Labels 102
Networking 103
Newspaper Clippings 104
No Gloves 104
Outside Shower 104
Packing to Move 105
Paint 106
Painting 106
Paint Colors 106

Paint Rollers 107

Paint Tray 107

Pantry 107

Paper Cups 108

Party Planning...108

Peroxide 109

Picnic Basket...109

Pictures 110

Picture Frames 110

Pillows...110

Pet Supplies 111

Pens, Pencils, and Markers 111

Place Markers 111

Place Mats 111

Plastic Containers..112

Potluck..112

Power Strip 113

Proof of Valuables for Insurance Purposes.................113

Quick Fixes...114

Reading Glasses 117

Recipes for Household Cleaners.................................117

Refrigerator...119

Reflective Vest...119

Rent It 120

Ride to School...121

Salad Spinner 121

Sales Rack...121

Sandpaper 122

Sandwiches 122

Scarfs, Ties, and Belts 122

Seasonal Clothes 123

Seasonal Cleaning 123

Security Systems with Recorders 124

Sewing Kit 124

Shampoo 125
Sheer Panel or Curtains 125
Sheets 125
Shoes 126
Shoe Caddie 127
Shovels 127
Silk Plants 127
Silver 128
Simple Green Cleaner 128
Soap Dispensers 129
Statements 129
Stickers 129
Storing Small Electrical Appliances 130
Storing Christmas Decorations 130
Storage Room and Tools 131
Sugar 131
Suitcases 132
Sweaters 132
Tabletops 132
To-do List 132
To Pit Cherries 133
Tools 133
Toothbrush Holder 133
Towels 133
Trash Cans 134
Transporting Food 134
Travel Bottles 134
Tuna 135
Umbrellas 135
Vacuum Fix 136
Vehicle 136
Velcro 137
VHS Tapes 137
Vintage Online Finds 137

Vents 138

Wagons 138

Walls 139

Warranty Papers 139

Water Key 140

White-canvas Shoes 140

Who Do I Call 140

Who Gets What When I'm Gone............................141

Windows 141

Wicker...142

Wiper Blades 142

Wire Storage Baskets 142

Work Clothes...142

Yard Clutter 143

Yard Sales 143

Ziploc Bags...144

Checklist..145

Bedroom Checklist...145

Great Room, Den, or Living Room Checklist.........146

Kitchen Checklist 148

Restroom Checklist 149

Pet Checklist...150

Monthly Checklist 151

Yearly Checklist 151

Yearly Planner 152

Index 155

Acknowledgments

To my family and every woman, who wants to take control of the clutter and disorganization in your life.

After much research, I am positive that I chose the right self-publishing company. Xlibris has been a wonderful experience; I would highly recommend Xlibris to anyone who is considering self-publishing.

I would like to thank Xlibris for publishing **The Polished Woman** and for all the hard work that was involved. I would especially like to thank Kristal Rodriguez for not giving up on me when I was trying to decide on a publishing company. The dedicated employees of Xlibris have done an outstanding job with the layout of the cover and the copy-editing team was a pleasure to work with. Their patience and knowledge is priceless. Vanessa, if ever I publish again, I hope to get you on the copy-editing team. You were and are a blessing to me. I would like to thank Sam Daniels, Roy De la Cruz and Glenda Lewis for all of your hard work.

Thank you . . . from the bottom of my heart,

Angie Massengill

Dedication

I would like to dedicate this book to my husband, Rick, who has been my strength and who has supported me in my every endeavor. You have stood by me and believed in me when I didn't believe in myself. You have loved me unconditionally and I love you more than words can say. To my mother-in-law Carol for your love, guidance, and support for loving me as your own. To my aunt Peggy for always giving me confidence and being my number one fan for always knowing when something was wrong and for loving me. To my beautiful daughter Jennifer you are smart, funny, and talented. I am so proud of you and your accomplishments. Thank you for coming up with the name and cover for this book. To my handsome son William I am so proud of you and your accomplishments. You have a brilliant mind. To my son in-law Jason I am so proud of you I love you as my own. To my brothers, Danny thank you for your tips on painting you should be writing a book you're a brilliant painter and have so much to share. To Steven and James for always being there and for your love and support. To my sister Cathy for your tips on yard sales, estate sales, and flea markets. To my best friends who have always been beside me Tina, Tyler, Emily, and Pam. To my grandchildren, Mackenzie, Braden, and Jade when I'm no longer here, my tips can guide you. Last but not the least: to my grandmother "Gracie," father "Bill," and mother "Dinkie." I will miss you always.

Life Is Short

"One thing's for sure *(life is short)*. It will get away from you in the blink of an eye; so don't blink," as Kenny Chesney would sing.

In saying that we are all leaving this earth and we are taking nothing out with us. You're not taking your money or your things. Live each day as if it were your last. Treat people the way you would want to be treated. And always think before you speak.

Do the best you can with what you have and be thankful for you have it. Be thankful for your family; you only get one. Everything that I have written about in this book requires nothing, but your time and energy. It is simple everyday practices that could help you get organized.

Introduction

I hope that my book will help you get organized and make your life easier. I want this book to help guide my children and my grandchildren for generations to come.

Life can be very difficult especially if you're a wife, mother, and work a full-time job. *We wear many hats.* Think about it; we are wives, mothers, caregivers, teachers, coaches, housekeepers, gardeners, nurses, etc. We have a lot to do sometimes with little or no help at all. The ideas in my book, *The Polished Woman*, are ideas that I have incorporated into my daily routine. I am always trying to find ways to make life easier for me.

One big key in getting organized is a routine and sticking to it. People ask me all the time, "How do you do it?" Each time I tell them it's my routine. *Sounds boring, but it works for me!* You have to get organized first. I want to know, where everything is in my home. If my husband calls me, I want to be able to tell him where to find whatever it is that he is looking for. If everything is in order, he can do so without turning the whole house upside down.

When I leave in the mornings for work, my housework is already done. I want my home to be guest-ready at any given moment. You never know who might pop in or if you're met with an accident, and someone has to come into your home. If you are the one who is disorganized then this book is for you. You will also find that I have included some helpful Web sites throughout the book.

Note: I have no financial or commercial interest in any Web sites, products, services, or professionals mentioned in this book.

Rules to Live By

- Have you ever gotten up and thought, "I just don't feel like putting my makeup on." But you knew that you had errands to run? I have, and everyone has. Even if I don't feel like it, I won't leave home unless I'm together. Your first impression is the last impression: it says that I'm in control, and I have it together.

- When I get up if I don't fix my hair and put on my makeup, I already know it's not going to be a good day. I truly believe that the way we look plays a big part in how we feel. Try it, you might be surprised. Don't say to yourself this is a waste of time, this is something you're doing for yourself, if you look good you'll feel good.

- If everything is in order before I go to bed at night. When I go to sleep I'm getting a good night's sleep and I'm not thinking about it subconsciously.

- I can enjoy my first cup of coffee instead of rushing through the morning.

- Let your husband and kids always hear the last words from you that, you love them even if you're mad or upset about something.

- *The most important of all is to keep* "God in your life."

Too Many Projects

How many times have you started a project and didn't follow through with it? This is how things get disorganized or you start to feel out of control. A good example is, while I was in the process of writing this book I overloaded my plate. I started writing this book after my father passed away. My intent was to leave little notes and instructions for my kids, because at the time death was on my mind. I had just lost my father after a long illness. Before I knew it, I had filled so many pages that I decided to have it published.

So I would write for a while and stop for a while. I now understand the phrase "writer's block." Then I thought I will open a business. After being employed at one company for eighteen years, I was left to open an antique, home décor, and gift shop. Mind you I have a husband, and a son at home. I was taking care of my mother from afar. I had just lost my father and I wanted my house, yard, cars, and business to be picture-perfect. I guess one might think I am an OCD, no I am organized and I love my life! I opened my business two months later; I lost my mother and six months later, I lost my grandmother. Now I am really depressed for my business isn't doing what I think it should, so I decided after a year to relocate. Now it's worst than ever. I closed my business down and put everything into storage. I took a break.

My point in saying all of this is, we sometimes get too many projects going on at one time. I had to step back and take a look at all the projects and things going on and prioritize. I still have so many things I want to do and have this organized life and I will, because if it is on my mind I can't rest until I get it done. That would be like going to bed with a sink full of dirty dishes. Nothing will get done if you just think about it and you don't do something about. If you stay on the road, and are on the move all the time or you're sitting in front of the TV you can forget it. Make a list of all the projects you have going on, and prioritize if one of your projects is cleaning up your flowerbeds or cleaning out the storage room. Do it and get it off the to-do list.

Get Organized

The first thing you have to do is to get organized. Then get into a routine. Instead of saying "Oh, I will do that later." "Do it now." Take control don't let the things that need to be done drag you down. Start organizing and prioritizing once you make your mind up you'll look back and say, "Why didn't I do this sooner." Sit down; make a to-do list of all the things you want to accomplish.

Some experts believe that making a list is a waste of time. The reason is, sometimes we put more on the list than we can handle. Make a list of the thing you want to do. Every time you finish something on the list mark it off. At the end of the day make a list of all the things that you did accomplish, whether it was on the list or not still write it down. You will be amazed at what you did do.

Have you ever worked all day in and around the house, but looked around and thought, "I've been working all day, but I can't tell I've done a thing." This is where the list will help you. Clean out a closet or drawer instead of watching TV. If there is a movie you want to watch try to find something productive to do during this time. Do the laundry, work on your filing system, or clip coupons, you would be amazed at what you can do while watching TV.

If you get into a routine of doing your housework throughout the week, then your weekends are free. Most people let the housework pile up until the weekend. Now you're stuck cleaning the house over the weekend then something comes up, and you have to stop cleaning, it has piled up even more and now you have double the workload.

Working Together

Some people don't like to work by themselves. I personally don't mind, sometimes I can concentrate better if I am by myself, but everyone is different. It may be that if one person is working they feel as if they are doing all the work, and that it is an endless battle. My fix for this is, to make my list of things to do; for each person a list that is yours, mine, and ours. We all take our list and start working all the projects down. So that while I am taking care of my list, my husband can take care of his list, then we do together the "our list" it works well.

Tools to Make Life Easier

As you read along, you will find that I am a firm believer in making a to-do list, a filing system, clear Rubbermaid containers, labels, decorative containers, and bins. Anything that will help me stay organized and on top of things. I love to shop for these types of items at flea markets, estate sales, and yard sales. Why pay retail for things I can find for a buck or two at a yard sale?

Getting Started

This will not happen overnight. Don't get overwhelmed and think you can't do this because you can. Decide which room you will be starting in.

Plan

- Plan ahead, get all of your supplies together, set a date, and stick to it. First you need time, "So Make Time."
- Purchase four *clear Rubbermaid bins* and trash bags. Get as much done on that day or weekend as you can. What you don't finish on that day or weekend pick back upon the next day or weekend or in the evenings, maybe take some vacation time and do this.
- Start with four bins. *Bin #1* will be used for the things that don't belong to the room you are working in, by placing the items in the bins; This will keep you from going from room to room.
- *Bin #2* in using for donations; list each item you are donating. You can take a percentage of the retail price you paid for the item as long as it is in good condition. *Note: Check your local and state regulations on donations. When that bin is filled, empty into a trash bag, and label the front of the bag as Donations.*
- *Bin #3* in using for trash. Every time you fill it up, empty it and start over.
- *Bin #4* will be for things you may want to give to someone you know or things you've borrowed and need to return.
- Do as much as you can in a weekend or a little each day.
- You will be most productive on a weekend. Stay focused on one room at a time. Don't think about what's ahead only on the project you're working on at that moment.

Starting Point

Decide where you want your starting point to be. After you have decided on that; that is what you need to focus on and stick to it. Don't start working in the bedroom and take something into the bathroom and forget what you were doing in the bedroom. Don't get sidetracked. Stick to the plan. It is a process.

- Find a neutral spot in the room you are working in, where you can line up the four bins. *Bin #1* is for the items that don't belong to the room you are working in. *Bin #2* is for the things you will be donating and *Bin #3* will be for trash. Only keep what you need. If you haven't used something or you have a duplicate of that item, get rid of it. *Bin#4* will be for things you may want to give to someone you know or the things you've borrowed, and need to return. Don't move it to another part of the house.
- Maybe you want to donate these items. The items that you will place in the bins are going to be the things that you have removed from the room, which you no longer want, need, or just doesn't belong in there. A good thing to remember, when you start the process of getting organized, is that all like-items are stored together (example) office supplies with office supplies; tools with tools; cleaning products with cleaning products, etc.
- Find a starting point such as the closets. A good rule of thumb is if you haven't worn a piece of clothing in the last six months to a year, get rid of it. A good way to see what you are wearing and how often is to turn all of your clothes hanger around backward, every time you wear a piece of clothing hang it back up, but this time you will be hanging it the right way in the closet. As you start going through the clothes separate seasonal clothes. As long as you are going through all the clothes, now this would be a good time for any that you might want to donate. Add those clothes to the donation bin. When donating items donate only the good items. Throw away anything that is stained, worn or missing buttons. As you fill up the bins have some heavy-duty trash bags handy, so you can empty the bins as need. After you have organized the closet, start on the

chest of drawers, now the clothes for that room have been organized.

- Linen's such as sheets, blankets, bedspreads, comforters, and pillows, etc. Find a spot for these items where they are altogether in one location. Now would be a good time to go through these items or donate what you no longer need.
- Remove anything from the top of the dresser and nightstands that doesn't belong; only keep bedroom items on the dresser and nightstands, make it cozy and inviting.
- Start with the bathroom by going through all the drawers and cabinets; take out anything not needed there, not pertaining to toiletry's or cosmetic's.
- All cleaning supplies should be in the laundry room or under the kitchen sink.
- Dirty clothes should be stored in the laundry room out of sight. Put two clothes hampers in the laundry room. One for whites and the other for colored clothes. Train everyone to place their clothes in the proper hamper; this will also help with starting a load of clothes. They're already there and you won't have to search the house for all of the dirty clothes.
- Start with the kitchen, clean up the pantry, and organize it. So when you open it, you can see what you have at a glance; make room for your spices in your pantry or find a cabinet that is for spices only, this is really helpful around the holidays when you start your holiday cooking. This will also help you when you're making out the grocery list.
- Clean out all the kitchen cabinets, put everything in order starting with your everyday dishes, and place them so that it is functional. This would be a good time to donate anything that you no longer use or the things you have duplicates of.
- Make a space for all of your mixing bowls, serving bowls, etc.
- Make a space for all of the plastic bowls with lids and misc. items.
- Put all pots and pans in one location.

- Clean all of the cabinet drawers out and get rid of anything that is not needed; only kitchen items need to be in the kitchen.
- Make one drawer in the kitchen for misc. items, such as pens and notepads.
- Clean the cabinets under the kitchen sink and get rid of everything except cleaning supplies.
- Keep all of these items, such as dishtowels, potholders, etc., in one location; put in a drawer or find a pretty basket to put them in.
- Separate daily placemats from the seasonal placemats. Find a place that is functional. You can also hang them on a hanger in a closet.
- As you are going through each room cleaning and getting organized any papers you come across put into a box or some kind of container and go through these things while you are watching TV, that would be a good time to start a filing system.
- All books organized together by category.
- All photo albums, pictures, and scrapbooks, if they are not complete, keep in a container with a note labeled to be done at a later date. This would be a good project to work on if you are having any kind of surgery that requires bed rest, or while you're watching TV.

There is a lot in keeping your home organized and orderly, it's all about getting it organized, getting in a routine and sticking to it. Be creative, have fun with it, and make it comfortable for you and your family.

To be Organized is a Lifestyle Change

This is something you have to do every day. What I mean by that is in order to stay on top of things; you have to discipline yourself in picking up things every day. This can't be something you do when it gets out of control, and you can't see the floor. All the clothes are dirty, the mail is piled up, and you can't see the kitchen table. Get everyone in the family involved; get them into a routine of picking up after themselves. Start by allowing yourself thirty minutes in the morning, this means for you getting up earlier, so if you need to be up by 6:00 a.m., then you need to get up at 5:30 a.m. Use the extra thirty minutes for picking up and straightening up things around the house, such as making the beds, pick up anything that is out of place; fluff the pillows, take the trash out, and the objective is to make sure things are guest ready before you leave in the morning for work or school. You want to be more organized, but it's not going to happen unless you make some changes. This has to come from within. It has to be something you want. It may be that you have to train everyone in the house to do this. I don't know about you, but I can't function in disfunction and honestly it can't be healthy.

If you have the attitude, "I can't do this, because no one else is helping me," you have it all wrong. Take charge, you want to be organized, don't wait for someone to do it for you or help you, you're not needy or helpless. I don't want to wait for and be at the mercy of someone else. If you want to clean up the storage room, do it. Plan out what you want to do, take the whole month. The first weekend, tackle the yard and flowerbeds; the second weekend, tackle the storage room; and the third weekend, tackle the house. Sooner or later everyone will get that you're ready for the lifestyle change.

Get into a Routine

You are probably thinking that "I don't have anything to do," but be organized (not so). I worked a full-time job for eighteen long years, a very demanding job; but I took care of the house, kids, parents, husband, and the list goes on and on. You will look back and think, "How did I do everything and keep it together." Once you get everything in order and get into a routine, the next step is to always stay a step ahead of the game. Instead of getting up in the mornings and trying to decide what you are going to wear to work or school, figure that out the night before.

Fix all the lunches, gather all the backpacks, coats, hats, and gloves and have them ready. Have the dishwasher already unloaded and ready to reload. Set the coffee pot the night before. All these little things make a difference when you're trying to get ready for work and get the kids ready for school. Anything you can do the night before will put you ahead of the game.

What Stays and What Goes

Pick a weekend that you can devote all your time to. Make up your mind you are really going to do it this time. If you don't think you can do it hire it done, sometimes when an outsider comes in, there is no emotional attachment to the items you are getting rid of. If you decide to do it yourself, you must stick to it. The first thing to remember is you have to make a mess in order to get organized. So this means taking apart each room piece by piece. Decide on the room you want to start with.

Doesn't belong: Bin #1

- Start with one section anything that doesn't belong to the room you are working for and add it to *Bin #1*.

Donate these items: Bin #2

- Anything that you want to donate, add those items to *Bin #2*. When the bin is full; empty it into a box, label the box, and set it aside. Make a list of each item in the box, tape the list to the box.

Trash: Bin #3

- If there are things you are throwing away, put those items in *Bin #3*. Have the large contractors bags handy as you fill the bin with trash, empty it into the large contractors bags.

Specific people/things to return: Bin #4

- Bin #4 is for things that you want to give to specific people or the things you have borrowed and need to return. After you have gone through everything, now would be a good time to deep clean this room or rearrange the furniture.
- Use the checklist for each room located at the back of this book. Once you have determined of what you are keeping and what you are getting rid of, the worst part is over with. Now you can start organizing and you're on your way to being organized. *Note: here is a list of things to have on hand before you start.*
- *Four Rubbermaid bins*
- Boxes: Empty the bins into the boxes, tape up the box, and write on the box what the contents are and where it's going, such as donations, maybe you have someone in mind to give these items to, or these items could be sold in a yard sale.
- *Tape/tape gun*

- *Permanent marker*
- *Contractor bags* for the things you are throwing away.
- *All cleaning supplies*

Note: Make sure you itemize anything that you donate. List all the things you are donating, you can write that off on your taxes. As you are itemizing write the retail price of the item, when you purchased it. You are allowed a percentage of the original retail price you paid for that item on your taxes. Please don't itemize junk. *Check the local laws in your state as the laws do change from year to year.*

Storage Room

If the storage room is out of control the simplest way would be to purchase four tarps or a large roll of plastic. If you have some old sheets, use them instead of buying the tarps or plastic. They are a little on the pricey side. Spread them out in the yard.

- *Tarp #1 is to keep items.*
- *Tarp #2 is to donate items.*
- *Tarp #3 is to sell items.*
- *Tarp #4 is to trash items.*

- Now you're ready to start the process of cleaning up the storage room, after everything has been pulled out and separated.
- Sweep out the storage room. Now would be a good time to hang any Peg-Boards, hooks, and or add cabinetry.
- Now you are ready to start putting things back in place.
- Put all like-items with like-items, such as sports equipment, tools, and automotive.
- When you're finished with it the only thing that should be there is the items you are keeping.

- The tarp that has the donated items should be donated, and not placed back in the storage room or the house. Make a list of everything you are donating for tax purposes.
- The tarp that has the sell items should be boxed up and labeled to be sold, plan on having a sale soon, if not donate or give to someone who could use the items.
- Last but not least, the tarp that has the trash items. Throw those items away.
- Save your tarps or plastic to use later for painting projects or you could use it as a cover if you have equipment outside.

The Outside of Your Home
Is as Important as the Inside

Have you ever been just driving along and see a house and it looks as if it has never been mowed, the flowerbeds have never been weeded, and clutter is everywhere? I have. Not only does it look bad it brings down everything around it. It affects your property value; it maybe that you don't know where or how to start the process of getting organized. If you are reading this and thinking that this sounds like me, you can use this book to guide you into the organized life you're wanting. Once you start organizing,

- you will feel better,
- you will be in control,
- you will not mind if someone pops in for a visit,
- if you have kids, you won't mind if your kids have their friends over because everything is in order and they are no longer worried about being embarrassed,
- if you have a spouse that's always complaining that things are always in a mess, there's no need to complain now you're organized and in control.

No Place Like Home

"No Place Like Home" is our saying. When we get home, it doesn't matter where we've been. When we walk in the front door, we're saying there is no place like home. The reality is everyone is different; you don't have to have a lot of money to be organized. Your home is what you make it. It doesn't matter if you live in a mansion or a mobile home. It doesn't matter if you're rich or poor. It's what's in your heart, mind, and what motivates you. You can sit around and do nothing or you can get up and do something about it. The only one who can change things is you. I know when I have everything in place and in order, I then feel like I am in control of all situations. Sometimes just moving one thing around will motivate me.

Hints, Tips, and Tricks

Address Labels

Address labels can save you time. Keep some of these in your purse. The next time your name and address are required, use the label instead of handwriting it.

- These are great for having films developed.
- For banking such as saving and withdrawal slips.
- If you have monthly bills and you have to use your envelopes to mail the bill go ahead and get them ready ahead of time, make up enough to carry you through the rest of the year. Buy the forever stamps just in case the price changes.

Aging Parents

At some point in our lives, we have to care for our parents when they become ill or can no longer do for themselves. There is a wealth of information out there and resources to help caregivers with information on legal, medical, financial, and support issues. Here are a few good places to start.

- *Administration on Aging:* (www.aoa.gov) Provides caregivers and their parent's information on various services including elder rights.
- *Area Agency on Aging:* This government program provides a national network of social services. See (www.n4a.org) (National Association of Area Agencies on Aging) or call 1-800-677-1116 for your local agency.
- *Family Caregiver Alliance* (www.caregiver.org): Offers programs at national, state, and local levels to support caregivers.
- *AARP* (www.aarp.org): Membership organization for people aged fifty and older provides numerous benefits to members.
- *Eldercare Locator* (www.eldercare.gov): A service of the U.S. Administration on Aging; links caregivers with senior services.
- *National Academy of Elder Law Attorneys* (www.naela.org): Provides searchable database to assist in finding an elder-law attorney.
- *Medicare Rights* (www.medicarerights.org): Independent sources of health-care information and assistance for people with Medicare.
- *National Hospice and Palliative Care Organization* (www.nhpco. org): Offers information on end-of-life issues and state-specific advance directives.
- *Nursing Homes* (www.medicare.gov/nhcompare): Provides detailed information on the past performance of every Medicare- and Medicaid-certified nursing home in the country.

Note: I have no financial or commercial interest in any Web sites, products, services, or professionals mentioned in this book.

Air Conditioner Filters

Keep a six-month supply of air filters for your air conditioner on hand. This helps with dust control. This will also help extend the life of your air conditioner. You can purchase the filters that can be changed every three months. Write the date on the filter, so you won't forget when you changed it last. There is also a five-year air filter. I have two. I change out my five-year filter every month. I rotate them each month, I take the filter out, and I wash it with the water hose. I'll let it air dry, and I store it until the next month.

Air Mattress

If you are limited in space, keep an air mattress handy. They make a comfortable bed, and this will eliminate anyone from sleeping on your sofa. There are different sizes to choose from depending on your needs. Don't rule out air mattresses for emergencies. You can use your air mattress as a floating device in case of a flood.

Antiques

Have you ever been looking for a unique item for your home, or a gift? I have found some of my most treasured items at Antique Malls. You would be amazed at what you can find in them. I also seek the smaller specialty shops. Yard sales and estate sales are another way of finding unique items; sometimes you're lucky enough to find a true antique treasure. But you have to be the early bird or you'll miss out because the antique dealers have beaten you to it.

Attic Storage

Attics are sometimes very difficult to get in and out of. So the less you have to go up and down the stairs the better. I found that if you label each box or clear Rubbermaid, and know what is in the box before you bring it down, it would make for a less dreadful task. Write or type each item that is in the box and put that list in a sheet protector, then tape that list to each box. Each time you add an item or remove an item from the box, don't forget to add or remove that item from the list on the box or clear Rubbermaid.

Baby Food Jars

Instead of throwing away the empty baby food jars, use it to store small items such as nuts, screws, or nails. Glue the baby food jar lid to the underside of a shelf or cabinet, and then screw the jar to the lid. Any size jar with a lid will work.

Backpacks

Don't throw that backpack away. Use it to store coloring books, crayons, doll clothes, children's books, anything small that would fit in there. Last year's gloves, mitts, or hats.

Backyard Barbecues

The next time you have a picnic, to keep away the uninvited guest such as ants, slip a Ziploc baggie on each leg of the table, securing it with a rubber band. Place each leg of the picnic table in a small pan of water. Ants can't swim. There's no way for them to get onto the table. After the picnic, don't forget to remove the table legs from the pans of water.

Bar

Here is a list of the things you need for a well-stocked bar. It will be expensive to stock your bar, the first time. Plan on spending $300 and above depending on the brands you purchase.

Liquor
- Bourbon
- Gin
- Rum (light)
- Scotch (blended)
- Tequila (white)
- Vermouth (dry)
- Vermouth (sweet)
- Vodka

Wine
- Red
- White

Beer
- Light
- Dark (import)

Mixers
- Cola (variety)
- Ginger ale
- Club soda
- Sparkling water
- Tonic water

- Cranberry juice
- Orange juice
- Pineapple juice

Garnishes
- Limes
- Lemons
- Olives (green pitted)
- Maraschino cherries
- Kosher salt

Accessories
- Long cocktail spoon
- Paring knife
- Peeler
- Cutting board
- Corkscrew
- Bottle opener
- Juice squeezer
- Standard shaker (metal on the top and bottom with a strainer)
- Jigger one ounce on one side, one and a half on the other side
- Bartending book
- Cocktail napkins
- Cocktail toothpicks
- Condiment tray

Glasses
- Highball glasses
- Martini glasses
- Wineglasses

Baskets

A good solution for baskets is to use them as a valance for your kitchen window. Hang a curtain rod, sturdy enough to support them. Leave enough space so the baskets don't rub the window. Hook on drapery rings with clips, attach to baskets and arrange. This is a great conversation piece. Baskets are my weakness, and I use them everywhere for books, magazines, towels, toys, and floral arrangements; the list could go on and on. Don't pass them up if you find them at yard sales.

Bed Rest

The doctor says no heavy lifting, but you'll go out of your mind. Here is a list of things you can do to keep yourself busy during this time. You could just lie in bed and watch TV or you could be productive. Make a list of all the things you would like to accomplish during this time. On your list, as you go through it, mark off what you have done. You will be surprised when you're finished. It always motivated me when I can mark the list done.

- Start that filing system.
- Organize those pictures.
- Get those home movies labeled and in order.
- Update your address book.
- Make a list of the frequently called numbers.
- Go through all of the newspaper clippings.
- Get all of your warranty papers together.
- Now would be a good time to get your proof of valuables list together.
- Update your cookbook.
- Get your 401(k) statements in order.

Anything you can do on this list will get you one step closer to being the organized person you want to be.

Beverages

The next time you're having an outside function, instead of purchasing a cooler, use your wheelbarrow. Line it with a festive vinyl tablecloth. Fill it with ice. It is shallow enough that everything is within view and easy to reach. If you don't own a wheelbarrow, use whatever you have in hand that would hold ice. Be creative and have fun!

Binders

Binders are a great way to store toy instructions, cards, electronic manuals, warranty papers, etc. Make each child a binder, and every time they get a new game, put the instructions, etc., in a sheet protector. Make a binder for 401(k) statements and bank statements always filing the latest statement on top. Note: You will need a hole puncher.

Birthday Cards

This is a good project when the doctor orders bed rest. Make a list of everyone's birthday for the year. Make a note beside each name, so when you're shopping for that special card, what the occasion is, mark birthday, anniversary, graduation, etc., and keep all occasion cards in hand just for emergencies. For the cards you receive, get a binder and some sheet protectors and the cards that you want to keep, slide them in the sheet protectors. You will be able to see the front, back, and the inside.

Blankets

Blankets that you don't use everyday, keep in zipper bags. If you don't have closet space, you could put them under your bed, and if you are really limited on space, you could remove your mattress and lay them between your mattress and box springs. You could be creative and put some of the decorative ones on quilt racks or you could hang them on the wall. Look at flea markets or yard sales for a cedar chest or trunk.

Books

If you collect books, display them on the coffee table, side table, or nightstand. Place an object on top of them or add a small floral arrangement on top. For the books in a bookcase stand, part of them up and lay some of them down, set a figurine on them. Another way to store them is in the subject order of the book. (For example, decorative books, how to books, misc. books, and cookbooks, etc.)

Boots

To hold the shape of your boots, tuck an empty soda bottle inside them. The plastic container will keep the leather from drooping over and getting a crease (your closet will look more organized). "Not only are you keeping your boots in shape, you are now recycling." Another way is to save the paper that comes in handbags. Instead of throwing it away, use it to stuff your boots or shoes to hold the shape.

Broom

A tennis ball is great for removing scuffs marks from tile floors. Cut a slit in a ball and slip it onto the top of your broom handle. Another good use for tennis balls is on walkers to keep from scuffing the floors put two on the front. Are you always afraid that you are going to hit the wall in the carport or garage when pulling in? Pull your vehicle into position in the carport or garage, from the ceiling take a string and tie it around the ball and let it drop down onto the windshield. When you pull in now, you will pull in until the tennis ball stops on your windshield.

Building a New House

Building a new house is a huge undertaking. You have three options: you can build it yourself, contract it out yourself, or have a builder do all the work for you. Either way it's a process, and needs a lot of patience, money, and time. We had our house built, and we decided to get a builder to do all of the work. There are so many details that go into building a house. The tips I would like to share is to make sure if you get a builder to build your house, make sure you and your builder know the codes in your area—each state is different. This is very important!

- Make sure you have thoughtout every aspect of your house. Make your home unique to you and your family's needs.
- Make sure that your builder provides you with a copy of the blueprint of your house, study it.
- Think about gas vs. electric.
- How many wall receptacles that has to be put in regarding code enforcement or how many extra ones you would like, also think about floor receptacles for furniture placement. Don't forget the outside receptacles in the front and back of your home.

- How does all of your venting such as dryer vents have to be placed in regards to code enforcement?
- We thought ahead and included extra wiring for a generator; we lose power frequently. We were thinking ahead of time: What if we have another Ice Storm? How would we stay warm?
- Do you want gas logs or a wood-burning fireplace? Or a fireplace at all.
- Make sure the builder is a quality builder, and that he uses the same contractors over and over. If a builder is using the same contractors over and over, then they know what the builder expects from them.

Our house plan had three different plans, built around a kitchen and master bath. It was built with our needs and wants in mind. Give it a lot of thought and plan ahead of time. The most important thing in building is to make sure that your builder has a good reputation and track record, and that the builder doesn't need your money upfront. Research the builder, ask questions, read reviews, and look at some of the homes that they've built in the past. Make sure your contract covers everything.

Business Cards

Business cards are good to keep for reference, but are easily lost or misplaced. Keep a Rolodex file just for business cards. Each time you get a business card, staple it to the Rolodex file card in alphabetical order. If the Rolodex file has the protective cover that covers the file card, slide it in place. When receiving a fax, cut out the business name and fax number and staple that information to the Rolodex card.

Buttons

How many times have you purchased a blouse and there was an extra button attached to it? Or you have found them in the washing machine? Put that button in a container or decorative box. The next time you lose one, you have a match. Buttons can also be used in many creative ways for crafting projects. If you have vintage clothes and you are throwing them away instead of donating them, take the buttons off. Then throw the clothing away. You would be amazed at what buttons are going for on eBay.

Cards and Letters

If you're like me, all cards and letters hold special meaning. I always want to keep them. The decorative hatboxes work well, and they are stackable. If you don't have the hatboxes, you could store them in the large Ziploc baggies. Also the cards that you receive, that are too pretty to put away in a box; put them in a picture frame to display.

Make a scrapbook for your special cards. Slide the card into a sheet protector. This way you can see both sides or find a pretty box with dividers labeled husband, son, daughter, etc.

Carpets

To keep your carpets looking like new, use area rugs, especially in high-traffic areas. There are a lot of decorative throw rugs and area rugs in different shapes, sizes, and colors to pick and choose from.

CDs

Put CDs in alphabetical order by artist. Keep holiday CDs separated from the everyday CDs. You can always add to your collection by looking at yard sales, flea markets, and estate sales for these items. There are many different style cases, and it depends on your taste and style. You can mount the case on the wall or let it stand freestyle. If you're looking for CDs, you can swap your old CDs at www.zunafish.com.

Note: I have no financial or commercial interest in any Web sites, products, services, or professionals mentioned in this book.

Ceiling Fan Blades

If you want to do something different with your ceiling fans, paint the blades the color of the walls. The only expense you will have is your paint and time.

Ceiling Fans

For the dust that collects around the motor of the fan, you can use your hairdryer to blow the dust off. You can also use a vacuum cleaner with attachments, or just the old-fashioned feather duster.

Cell Phones

Have you ever left home and realized that you had forgotten to recharge your cell phone? This has happened to me. Keep a car charger in the car. Occasionally we all update our cell phones. We want the latest and greatest version, so we go and get a new one.

Donate your old phone or give it to someone that could use it. There are a lot of organizations such as www.wirelessfoundation. org this organization is for domestic violence victims. This information should be passed on to everyone.

- How to disable a stolen cell phone? To check your cell phone's serial number,
    - key in the following digits on your cell phone press * # 06 #.
    - A fifteen digit code will appear on the screen. The number is unique to your handset.
    - Write it down and keep it somewhere safe.
    - If your cell phone gets stolen, call your service provider, give them the number, and they can disable your cell phone. You are without a cell phone and now the thief is too.
    - Not even changing the SIM card will help them. The cell phone is now useless.
- Every time we call for directory assistance, we are charged anywhere from a $1 to a $1.75 that can add up over a month. There is a *FREE 411 number*. Program it into your cell phone. You can call at *1-800-373-3411 or 1-800-FREE 411* for assistance without incurring any charges.
- *National Do Not Call List* telemarketing companies call usually just as you're sitting down for dinner. Now they can call you on your cell phone. To prevent this, call the following number from your cell phone. It will only take a minute, and it will block them from calling you for five years. The number is *1-888-382-1222*. Do this from your cell phone and your home phone.

Note: I have no financial or commercial interest in any Web sites, products, services, or professionals mentioned in this book.

Certificate of Authenticity

If you collect dolls or any collectibles, the Certificate of Authenticity can easily get misplaced. Keep the certificate in a binder, the certificate has the name of the item and the number, as well as other information about the item. On a post a note write the date you purchased the doll or collectible and the amount. So if you are a collector, this is a good way to reference back.

Chest of Drawers

Chest of drawers are good for a lot of things besides just clothes. You could use that space for items that you wouldn't normally use daily, such as heirloom's that have been past down. Sheets, tablecloths, and anything that you want to keep and wouldn't want to be use daily.

Cleaning Supplies

Keep cleaning supplies in one place. Find a small storage container for storing, cleaning brushes, and small items. Purchase a clear Rubbermaid container that will fit under your sink to store all of your cleaning supplies in. Then if you ever have a leak, all you have to do is pull the Rubbermaid container out. Always store like-items with like-items.

Clear Containers

I am a big fan of clear containers. They are great for storing items such as clothes and holiday decorations. This is especially good for people that are visual. Plus you can see what's in the container before opening it. Clear Ziploc bags are also good. I use clear Ziploc baggies to store and separate items such as cosmetics, loose change, buttons, batteries, and small toys.

Clothes

Monday mornings are hectic because we have to go back to work and school. Set aside time the evening before and have the kids select their school clothes for the week. Hang the entire outfit on hangers labeled Monday–Friday. Or put a sweater hanger in the closet, label each compartment, have them place their outfits in there along with the matching accessories such as underwear, socks, and anything that goes with it. Find and use what works best for you. Then you mom makes sure that everything coordinates, so when they get ready to leave, you know everything matches.

Clothing for Emergencies

I try to always be prepared no matter what the situation, be it expected or unexpected. Take a look at everyone's dress clothes in case of an emergency. When something tragic happens, you may not be thinking clearly. Keep these basic clothes articles in hand just for that reason.

- Black dress
- Black suit
- White blouse
- Black and white bra
- Black and white slip
- Black or off black hosiery

- Black high-heel shoes or black pumps
- Black handbag or clutch

For the men keep:
- A basic black suit
- White shirt and white T-shirt
- Tie with a tie tack
- Black-dress shoes
- Black socks
- Black-dress belt

Also think about the kids, keep a cute outfit and shoes for the girls; and for the boys, keep a nice pair of pants, belt, shirt, matching socks, and shoes. You never know when you may have to have these items.

Clothes You no Longer Wear

What to do with them is the question. Clear Rubbermaid containers is the answer: they are airtight, durable, and stackable. Pack up what you want to keep. Label the top of the Rubbermaid with the contents. So if you are looking for an item, you don't have to open every Rubbermaid to find what you're looking for. You may have clothes that don't fit anymore. They're either too large or too small, but you're not ready to let go of yet. Pack them up; label the container, with the reason why they are packed up, put the size on there and any other information.

Another solution would be to hang all your clothes up backwards. Every time you wear an article of clothing, hang your clothes back up, the right way at the end of six months; toss any pieces that are still hanging in the wrong direction. It's really a good way to see which clothes you are wearing, and which you're not. Clothes that still have the price tags on them, and you want to get rid of instead of putting them in a yard sale, take them to a consignment shop for resale. Clothes you are throwing away remove all the buttons and save them. You never know when you may need one.

Closets

Have you ever gone to your closet, and you didn't know where to start looking? I like to know where everything is. I found that if you sort all like-items together into sections, it is much easier to find what you are looking for. For example, sort all long dresses together, all short dresses together. Separate all of your long sleeve shirts, short sleeve shirts, and sleeveless shirts. Do the same thing for all of your blouses in the same order or you could separate by color.

Separate your dress slacks. Separate your blue jeans. If you are one that has every color in jeans, and have more than one color of each, you could sort them by color. If you are one that is always going up and down in your clothes size, you can separate by size. Get closet tags, you can order them from www.clutterdiet.com a set of twelve for approximately $12. They snap onto your closet rod and come with preprinted labels.

Note: I have no financial or commercial interest in any Web sites, products, services, or professionals mentioned in this book.

Clutter within Clutter

It's everywhere in the drawers, on the counters; small items such as ink pens, pencils, loose change, lighters, scrap paper, business cards, nuts, bolts, screws, hair bows, small toys, coral, everything you find together into one bin. As you're cleaning every time, you find small items, place it in the bin. After everything is organized and you're ready to put everything away that you've collected into the bin, sort everything by category and put these items in their proper places.

Coats

We never have enough room in our closets for coats. The coat racks that hang on the wall work well. Look for the decorative ones; put one on each side of the entryway door. Look for retail stores that are going out of business, and purchase clothing racks and hangers. This is good for the clothes you want to store. Use that rack for extra coats and other misc. items that you don't want to hang in the closet. You can also use these racks when you are having a yard sale. You could use the stand-alone coat rack if you can give up the space, but then you have to worry about it tipping over. Donate your extra coats to Coats for Kids. Or look for charities in your area.

Cookbook

So your cookbook is a mess! You've collected this recipe, and that recipe it has no order, they're just in there. Cooking isn't enjoyable because you can't find the recipe that you were looking for. Do you print off recipes from the Internet? If so, make a notebook just for Internet recipes, put each one of them in a sheet protector, and call your cookbook, "Cookbook.Net." Handwritten recipes could be filed in a recipe box. Staple the recipe to the index card then file it. You could also make a file on your computer, and add it to your desktop. There are some pretty cookbook stands out there, display one of them open on the counter.

Cold Days and Nights

If you live in a mobile home, make sure you have good insulation in your home. Your pipes could freeze and burst. Always winterize before it gets cold, making sure all pipes are wrapped and you have good underpinning up. On really cold days and nights, let your water drip, a slow drip in each sink and bathtub in your home. Also open all of the cabinets to the sinks, so some of the heat can get in there. Place a washcloth at the bottom of the sink or bathtub; this will eliminate the dripping sound. (Note: Do not cover the drain.)

Colored Hangers

To keep everything organized, assign each family member a different colored clothes hanger. It will be easy to see which clothes belong to whom. Make a list of who you assigned what colored hanger to. Post it in the laundry area.

Cords

Having trouble locating the cords to the TV, VCR, or DVR? Tag both ends of the cord. Label each one. Label each cord with key tags.

Cosmetics on a Hot Day

On a hot summer day, have you ever tried to freshen up your makeup only to find that your lipliner and eyeliner have melted? This usually happens to me when I'm in my car. My fix for this is to turn the air conditioner on high, and stick my lipliner and eyeliner in the vent for a minute. Now I'm ready to freshen up.

Cosmetics

When I purchase a new product, if I don't like that product after I have purchased it, I keep it because I may change my mind later on about it. I like to keep my cosmetics that still have a little left in them because sometimes this can be a lifesaver. For example, "I lost my eyeliner. I have a backup because I kept my old eyeliner." Don't keep for too long. Makeup expires too. Don't throw away the product that you no longer want, give it to someone that could use it.

Crystal

One of my favorite things to collect is crystal. When I get ready to wash it, I'm always afraid that I will break it because it's so delicate. If you place a towel at the bottom of the sink, you will be less likely to break any pieces. After I have washed each piece, I let it air-dry on a towel. Another way is to fill a spray bottle with one part rubbing alcohol, and three parts water. Then spritz the crystal and wipe with a clean dry cotton cloth; for the crevices use a cotton swab.

Crystal Chandelier

Have you ever tried to clean a crystal chandelier? "It can be such a headache." Cover the surface below the chandelier; this will eliminate any of the cleaning solution from getting on the tabletop. Mix one part rubbing alcohol and three parts water in a spray bottle. After you spray the solution onto the chandelier, let it air-dry. If you find hard to reach spots, use a soft, natural bristle artist paintbrush or a fine pastry brush.

Curling Iron

To remove hairspray that has been baked onto your curling iron, first, unplug the curling iron, dip a cotton ball in rubbing alcohol, and wipe until clean, use a clean damp cloth when finished. This will remove the built-up hairspray. There have been times that I needed to take my curling iron with me, but I had just finished using it and it was still hot. My solution for this is to take a damp cloth and wrap it around the iron to keep from getting burned or burning something.

Decorative Storage Units

We never seem to have enough storage space in our restrooms. Find a decorative stand with drawers. Store items such as ribbons, bows, makeup, or any misc. items that you wouldn't want to be seen on the counters. Also use a pretty basket for bathroom tissue.

Decorating Styles

Everyone has their own decorating style, and there are so many different styles that it can be overwhelming. Then you start purchasing magazines, you find a style you like but now you're not sure. So you buy another magazine, then before you know it you're swimming in a sea of magazines and you can't remember which magazine you found the style you liked. A quick fix for this is to sit down with all of your magazines, clip out all of the styles that you like. Then separate them into categories. Keep them in a file for reference. Another way would be to make a scrapbook when you're finished, throw the magazines away or donate to a nursing home or doctor's office, etc. Remove your name and address by peeling the label off or mark through with a permanent marker.

Direct Deposit

If you are on direct deposit, you should be taking advantage of these bank's services. Go to your bank and ask about having a percentage of your payroll check deposited into your saving account each month. Most people set it up for the fifteenth and the thirtieth of each month.

Start up with an amount that you will be comfortable with. After you have subtracted the amount from your checkbook, now would be a good time to log that amount you are putting into your savings account, don't forget to add the interest that you've earned into your saving account book. At the end of the month, you will be balancing your checkbook and your saving account book. You will be so surprised to see how much you have saved, if you put it in there and forget about. It is like always having a nest to fall back on in case of an emergencie.

Digital Picture Frames

This is a neat way to give someone a gift. Purchase a digital picture frame, check to make sure it comes with a memory card. If it doesn't, purchase one and use that memory card in your digital camera, and take pictures that you want to share with the person you bought the digital picture frame for. After you've taken the pictures, insert the memory card into the digital frame, wrap up the gift and give it to them. This is great if you have loved one out of state.

I just recently done this. My husband's side of the family always has a family reunion in November. So while we were there, I made sure that I was in charge of taking all of the pictures. I took the memory card and I purchased a digital frame, I inserted the memory card into the digital frame and that was my father-in-law's Christmas gift. It was great and what a surprise!

Doctor

If you have a lot of medical problems and you have a long list of doctors, you may find this tip helpful. Make a list of each doctor with their address and phone number, and what you are being treated for. Have this list with you when you go to the doctor, so they can put it in your file. This is especially good when you're seeing a new doctor. The list should include by date order, each doctor that has treated you, all medications that you are taking, all insurance, and emergency contacts. Keep a copy for yourself and a copy for each of your doctors. This will keep you from filling in all of this information twice.

Documents

Keep all of your documents in one place at the end of the year, when it's time to file your taxes you have everything you need. This will keep you from searching for documents. Purchase the large 9½ × 12½ white or yellow envelopes. Put your documents such as all of the year's electric bills in date order with the name and total for the year on the front of the envelope, this will let you know at a glance what the contents are. You should have an envelope for all documents that you've been filing throughout the year. Store these documents in a clear utility tote that is 14½ × 17½ in size, they hold letter and legal-size files.

After you have filed your taxes, take the envelope that contains your tax information, file it in the utility tote with the date showing through on the outside, so you can see what year is in the utility tote at a glance. By keeping these documents in a utility tote you're cutting down on cardboard, which in turn cuts down on pest, and the utility tote is waterproof. I use them for everything; they are durable, stackable, and reusable.

Dog and Cat Food

Storing dog and cat food dry in the original bags, leaves an odor as well as an open invitation for pest. Put dog and cat food in airtight plastic containers. Not only will this eliminate the odor now, you won't have to worry about mice or bugs. You could also use metal or glass containers as long as they are airtight. If you use metal, before you fill the container with your pet's food, paint the bottom of the metal container with a clear sealant. This will help to keep the bottom from rusting.

Dresser Drawers

Keep undergarments separated such as panties, bras, and slips. Keep hosiery in plastic bags separated from everything else, and separate by color. Keep socks separated in a drawer for socks. Hang up pajamas and housecoats. Make a section in the closet for these items. Separate the blue, black, and brown socks. Keep the black socks separated from all the other colors because it is so easy to get the black and blue mixed up. Get into a habit of buying the same style. Keep all of the other colors such as blues and browns together. This helps them find what they are looking for. Keep white socks in a separate drawer, away from the colored socks.

Keep underwear in one drawer and T-shirts in another drawer. Keep a drawer for misc. items such as long johns and pajamas.

I know this sounds like a lot of drawers that you may or may not have, but the good news is that there are so many decorative cabinets that have drawer space. You could incorporate this in with your furniture to have the additional drawer space you didn't have before.

DVDs

Make a book of movies with your DVDs. You can make a book with a CD carrying case that zips. Each pocket will hold the insert from the DVD.

Use the DVD cover as the label for the movie. Insert the DVD behind the label. Now you have a book on movies.

Earrings

I keep all of my pierced earrings that I've lost either the back to the earring or the earring itself. I also try to find them at yard sales, flea markets, and thrift stores. I like to use them as thumbtacks instead of regular tacks. They are good decorative tacks and work well on the corky boards. Who knows you may get lucky and find the match.

Entryway

Have you ever gone to someone's home and had to wait for them to clear the path of shoes before you could get in the door? I have and it is very uninviting. Put a decorative trunk by the door for everyone to put their shoes in after they take them off.

Instead of everyone kicking their shoes off, get everyone in a habit of placing them in the trunk. This hides the shoes as well as eliminating them from walking onto the carpet with soiled shoes.

Emergency Contact List

Make a list of the people that you would want to contact in case of an emergency. Keep a copy by your phone and in your address book.

Other places you could post them.

- In your car
- In your purse
- In your billfold
- If you have a teenager driving, keep in the glove box of their car an emergency contact list in his/her billfold or purse always have an action plan in place with them discuss with them what to do if there were a disaster.
- Give a list to your family members
- Post on refrigerator

Emergency Grab-and-Go File

Having your medical information with you will speed up things in the Emergency Room. But you may be distracted as you head out the door or unable to gather it all. So in advance, create a file for each family member that includes

- A short medical history, including past surgeries or major problems
- Current medical conditions
- Doctors and their phone numbers
- Medications
- Immunizations
- Allergies (especially drugs, latex)
- Insurance information

If an emergency strikes before you've prepared a file, grab the patient's medicine bottles (if any and insurance information). It's also crucial to give a signed medical consent form for your kids to your babysitter or anyone, who might need to take the kids to the hospital. To print out medical forms go to www.pamf.org/forms under types of forms, select medical history forms there are pediatrics, adolescents/parent/guardian and adult form to choose from; print off, fill in, and file.

Note: I have no financial or commercial interest in any Web sites, products, services, or professionals mentioned in this book.

Emergency Kit for the Home

First, always have a plan in place with your family members. Each person needs to be aware of where to find the emergency kit. Items that you would want to include in your kit.

- Contact list
- First-aid kit
- Flashlights
- Batteries (all sizes)
- Candles
- Lighter or matches
- Radio/weather radio
- Small battery-operated TV
- Duct tape
- Roll of plastic or sheets
- Mask, gloves
- Money
- Water
- Nonperishable items such as canned meats, peanut butter
- Manuel can opener
- Handy wipe
- Hand sanitizer

Remember to check and replace items at least twice a year. Daylight savings time would be a good time to do this.

Emergency Roadside Kit

Keep an emergency kit in the trunk of your car or if you drive a truck, keep behind the seat. You never know when you might need one, this could not only help you, and it could also help someone else. You can purchase them ready to use, or you could make your own. Most kits have everything you would need; I added some additional items I wanted to keep in hand such as bottled water, batteries, flashlight, hard candy, wet wipes, and a blanket.

I like the tire inflators that charge on the cigarette lighter. You can purchase the chargers that can be charged at your home, after each use recharge. Design a kit that meets your needs. Also keep an emergency contact list in the console or in the glove compartment along with your insurance papers and registration.

Items to keep in car.

- Spare tire and jack
- Jumper cables
- Flares
- Tools
- Extra fluids such as oil, brake fluid, power steering fluid, transmission fluid, and water.
- Tire inflator
- Flashlight and batteries
- Bottled water
- Wet wipes
- Hand sanitizer
- Hard candy
- Blanket
- Contact list
- Registration
- Insurance papers
- Cell phone charger

Emergency Kit for Storm Shelter or Basememt

- Have a plan in place with each of your family member in case of hurricane, tornadoes, or thunderstorms. If you have a storm shelter take precaution and store these items there, you never know when you may need them.

- I keep all items stored in clear Rubbermaid because of the dampness and condensation. They are airtight, durable, and stackable.

> - Contact list
> - First-aid kit
> - Mask/gloves
> - Wet wipe, paper towels, and tissue
> - Hand sanitizer
> - Flashlights
> - Batteries (all sizes)
> - Battery-operated radio/weather radio
> - Small battery-operated TV
> - No candles in a small space
> - Blankets
> - Extra suit of clothes for each family member
> - Fold-up chairs
> - Battery-operated clock
> - Bottled water

- You can add to your emergency kit depending on you and your family's needs. I also keep a bag ready to take with me that has my important papers in case of disaster. Don't wait until a storm is upon you to decide, to start preparing think ahead every second counts!

Errands

Before you start out for the day to run your errands, sit down with a pen and paper and map out your route. Not only will this save your time, it will keep you from backtracking and will save time and gas, not to mention mileage on your car.

Fanny Pack

Fanny packs are a must. They are great to use if you're going to a flea market or yard sale. If you're working in the yard, you can keep your cell phone, keys, and anything else you might need in there. You have everything, you need right there on your waist. This way, your home is locked and secure while working outside, and you have your cell phone in case of an emergency.

Flea Markets

My sister is the flea market and yard sale queen. She never pays retail, and her home is filled with beautiful antiques. You never know what you will find at a flea market, everything from old photographs to your favorite collectables. These are the things to look for.

Before You Go:

- Do your research if you have something specific in mind, "visit antique shops that sell the type of items you're after." "Most dealers are happy to share their expertise."
- Compare prices online and bring along information to help you find what you are looking for.
- Make a list of how much you'd like to spend on each item you're looking for. Don't think that you can remember in your mind, because once you start shopping you can get overwhelmed because there is so much to look at. Bring enough money for those purchases—plus a bit extra.
- Carry cash, most vendors don't accept credit cards and many don't take checks.

Shopping Strategies:

- Look for color and character first. Next ask yourself, can I really use it? Will it accent or fit in with what I already have in my home?
- If you know in advance that you need a piece of furniture, assess the size of the space and bring a tape measure.
- For higher price items see if you can pay by check, and ask for a business card in case you want to purchase other pieces in the future.
- When you see something you want, don't hesitate or you may lose out. "Someone else will snap it up."

How to Bargain:

- Determine how much you are willing to pay, and don't pay more. Just walk away from it.
- Always be polite to vendors. They will be more likely to negotiate with you.
- When you buy several items ask for a package deal. "If I buy all three, will you come down on the price?"
- When the cost of the item is unfair, be prepared to walk away, no matter how much you love it.
- Vendors at the same market may have similar items at a different price. You have nothing to lose by approaching one of them, explaining that you saw the same item for less and asking if they are willing to negotiate.
- Keep your sense of humor, should a vendor reject your offer, smile and walk away, it just wasn't meant to be.

Also if you live in a small town, check and see if you have a once-a-month flea market. We have a first Monday flea market, which is held the last weekend before the first Monday of every month, excluding the winter months. We all get together and make a day of it.

Fireplace

Not only can you use your fireplace for warming your home in the winter. During the summer when it is not in use, make a large floral arrangement and put it in there, or use candles instead of wood, decorate the mantle.

Fireplace Odor

Place a shallow pan of baking soda in the fireplace overnight after you've cleaned out the ashes. The unpleasant soot smell will diminish.

Filing System

Every household needs a filing system. How many times have you looked for a bill you know that you've paid? How can you dispute it if you can't prove it? Make files that are easy to read. Make individual files. Make files for everything. Set up your filing system in alphabetical order. Set up your filing system always filing to the back; this will keep everything in date order. Before you file away that bill, always write paid and the date along with the check number.

Example of files:

- Mortgage note or rent
- Utility bill
- Phone bill
- Cable bill
- Car note
- Car insurance
- House insurance
- Health insurance. Note: If more than one insurance, make separate files
- Credit card. Note: If more than one credit card, make a file for each credit card that you hold
- Cell phone bill
- Newspaper bill
- Rebates
- Receipts
- Restaurant menus
- Doctor receipts/co-pays
- Warranty papers
- Newspaper clipping
- May want to order file
- Make yourself and every member of your household, a file as well as a misc. file for each member of your family
- Make your pets a file
- Car files
- Check stub file
- Report cards
- Marriage file
- Divorce file
- Property file
- Taxes file
- Coupon file
- Burial insurance or policies
- Purging file

The key in having a filing system that works for you is having all the files that you need and using it. Use two four-drawer filing cabinets, when I discover a need for a new file, I make it and add it to my files. Use one drawer for office supplies. I found that when I am paying my bills that if everything is right there such as envelopes, stamps, labels, stapler, staple puller, whiteout calculator, and ink pens. I don't have to keep getting up to find these items. After I have paid all the bills, I store all of these items in a small clear container with a lid. Now you've paid the bills, file them and you're done.

Flower Vases

It's difficult to wash a flower vase, especially if it has a thin neck. Drop a denture-cleaning tablet in the vase, fill with water, this should do the trick. Once the denture tablet dissolves, rinse it out. Also a baby bottlebrush works well.

For the Less Fortunate

Keep a bin in the storage room for items that you no longer need, use, or want; instead of throwing these items away. Find someone who is less fortunate to give these items to. I've always heard that one man's trash is another man's treasure. What may be old and used too you may really help out someone else in a less fortunate situation. Keep a list of all donations and file all documentation with your taxes at the end of the year.

Fresh Cut Flowers

Add floral food to a vase of water to nourish the blooms and fight bacterial growth. If you don't have any food packets handy, this homemade recipe works just as well: mix one quart of clean warm water, one tablespoon of bleach, and one fourth cup of lemon-lime soda.

Frequently Called Numbers

Set aside a day, and make a list of all of the phone numbers you frequently call such as the hardware store, wrecker service, post office, pharmacy, grocery store, doctor's office, and National Poison Control Hotline Number 1-800-222-1222. This will save you some time and will eliminate pulling the yellow pages out or calling information every time you need a phone number. Also add these numbers to your cell phone list.

Funeral

The next time you send your condolences, instead of sending fresh flowers, send something that can be taken home such as an Angel, silk flower arrangement, wreath, or a wall hanger. This is something that can be a keepsake for the family. Make a scrapbook, in the scrapbook place the newspaper obituary there along with funeral program and a picture.

Gardening Tools

Have you ever been working in your yard or garden and lost one of your gardening tools? I found that I spent more time looking for my gardening tools than working in the yard. So I painted the handles in a bright color, so I could see them. After I am finished with my gardening tools, I store them in a bucket of sand. I stick my gardening tools in the sand, which will take the dirt off of them. Now they are ready for the next use.

Note: Instead of throwing away your old knee-high socks, cut the feet off and slip them over your arms when weeding to help guard against scratches and poison ivy.

Gifts

Sometimes my husband has trouble deciding what to buy for me. To help him out, I keep a folder that has clippings of the things I would like in it along with a wish list that has my clothe's size, shoe sizes, and favorite perfumes.

He can easily pick a present for me, and I'm still surprised because I don't know which one he has chosen. Everyone in the family has a file, this makes shopping easier for a gift (1) they're getting something they want and (2) this makes it easy for you, because now you don't have to worry if they are going to like their gift.

Gifts for Unexpected Guest

Always be ready for the unexpected guest by having these items in hand just in case.

- One size fits all gloves for women
- Picture frames
- Two candles tied with a pretty ribbon
- Decorative soap

- Wallets for men, don't forget to put a dollar in there for luck
- Toys for girls or boys or a "socking with holiday candy"
- Box of candy

My granddaughter, Jade, always says, "Mamaw do you have a surprise for me?" I keep bubbles in hand for her.

Gift Bags/Boxes and Ribbons

When someone gives you a gift in a pretty bag, don't discard it, reuse it: You never know when you may need it. Purchase them when they are on sale. Fold all of your gift bags and store them inside a gift bag. Use another gift bag for all bows and ribbons. Also I like to look for pretty boxes; they are great for small items such as candles.

Gift-wrapping Paper

A good way to store gift wrap paper is to save your old panty hose. Cut the legs off the panty hose and slide your gift wrap roll into the panty hose leg. This will prevent it from unrolling. If you don't wear panty hose, use old socks, cut the foot off, and slide it over the paper.

Gift Tags

A simple fix for a gift tag is: if you have any leftover paint swatches from your recent kitchen or bathroom redo, take a swatch that matches the paper, cut a round tag from those colorful paint chips, punch a hole in it, and tie with a thin ribbon.

Girls' Night Out

Instead of hitting the bar, get together with all the girls and have a purse party.

- Everyone has a purse that they are tired of; turn it into a purse swap party.
- Have a jewelry swap party.
- Have a perfume party, swap perfumes.
- Redecorate your home instead of purchasing new home décor. Swap out with a friend.

There are many things you can do, not only are you having fun you've just done two things: one is, you're saving money and two, your husbands are not mad!

Grease Catcher

If you have lost or misplaced the tray that catches the grease to your George Foreman grill, use the top of an egg carton to catch the dripping grease. Throw it in the trash when finished. Just cut it to fit under the grill. The cleanup is a snap.

Grocery List

Have you ever gone to the grocery store and got home and realized that you didn't get what you had gone for or had duplicated an item that you already had? It is very costly, and why take up space for something you already have? Start taking an inventory of the items that you have in hand. Then make a list of the items that you need.

When you start your shopping, stick to your grocery list, mark it off as you go, this will keep you from either duplicating an item or buying on impulse. Never go to the grocery store when you're hungry. If you are hungry, you will think you want or need everything in sight. Also check at guest care at your local market for a printout of the store products and aisle numbers. If you ever have to send someone to the store for you, you can tell him or her the aisle number to go to.

Grocery Receipts

Have you ever wondered just how much money you spend at the grocery store for the year? I decided to keep track, so I made a sheet in excel listing all of the stores that I shop weekly. I made the sheet to work for me. I listed the thirty-one days, each store name, and how I paid; did I pay by check, debit, cash, or credit card? This is good for tracking purposes. So every time I make a purchase for groceries, I log the total on to the sheet. This is especially good if you're paying by debit; when you log in, the receipt in your checkbook or when you balance your bank statement, you can log your receipt then.

Guest Room

- Make room for your guest belongings; clear a dresser top, a dresser drawer or two, and some closet space. Leave a few hangers for shirts, pants, coats, or sweaters.
- Put a reading light and magazines on the nightstand. Along with bottled water and juices.
- In the guest bathroom, put out fresh towels and washcloths. Fill a basket with scented soaps, bath oils, fresh powders, and

lotions. Gather basic needs, your guest may have forgotten such as toothbrush, toothpaste, shampoo, conditioner, razor, shaving cream, and aspirin.

- Have a hair dryer just in case they forgot theirs.
- Other nice touches would be a picture of your guest, stationary, and pen.
- A nice candle that they could light while bathing.
- A nightlight for unfamiliar territory.
- If you have an extra coffee pot, set up a coffee station in their room, so your guest can make their coffee, just in case they're an early riser.

Handbags

A good way to keep all of your handbags together is to use a sweater bag. Separate evening bags, sports bags, and everyday bags; they are all right there together. Handbags with long shoulder straps can also be hung in your closet or placed on the top shelf of your closet. If you have high ceilings, you could add another shelf for extra space.

Hats and Gloves

A good way to keep from misplacing hats and gloves is to get a shoe caddy that hangs over the door, label each pocket with each family member's name. The clear shoeboxes are also good. Label the top of the box when the winter months are over, they are already packed and ready to be stored until next year. Be creative in using decorative containers or baskets.

Hedges

The next time it's time to trim the hedges, to eliminate cleanup time, try putting a sheet or a tarp down to catch all the clippings. Pickup all four corners at the same time empty into the trash can.

Heirlooms

Do you ever worry that your heirlooms might make it to a yard sale, estate sale, or flea market? To make sure that your heirlooms aren't mistaken for junk or clutter is to label it. A lot of times we pack away things and we forget about it, then something tragic or unexpected happens. Someone has to go through your belongings. If you have heirlooms that have been past down from generation to generation, make a note and attach it to that item. On the note include the history behind the heirloom; this will take a lot of the guesswork out of it.

Also if you have inherited an estate after the Will has been read, you look around and there is still a houseful of items. You don't know what to do with all these items, but at the same time you want to be fair about it with your siblings.

Purchase a card with colored stickers. Each person is assigned a color. Draw numbers to see who will go first. Starting with the kitchen, the person that starts off would then place the color sticker that they were assigned on the item they picked; that way everyone knows which items are theirs. Then go through each room until you're finished.

His and Her Storage Space

Everyone has things that have special meaning or things that they may want to keep for whatever reason. My husband and I each have our own space, and it works for us. If you have a storage unit that has two floors, give him the bottom and you take the top or vice versa. If you have a small storage room and or attic space, equally divide the space for both spaces, and that way he will have his space and you will have yours.

Holiday Preparation

Don't wait until the holidays are upon you to start thinking about it. Think and plan ahead. By doing so, you will be taking some of the pressure off you. You will be able to enjoy the holidays instead of dreading them. When you wait until the last minute, everything has been picked over. Around October, start planning your Thanksgiving dinner, every time you go for grocery shopping in October, start gathering your staples such as the things you'll need for baking your cakes, pies, etc, and anything else you may want to serve.

Make a list of each dish you want to serve. Think about what ingredients goes into each dish, check to see if you have the ingredients. Make a list and keep it in your purse and on the refrigerator. Do the same thing in November for Christmas dinner. Do this anytime you're planning an event or a get together.

Holiday Shopping

After Christmas, get a notebook or journal to keep track of the next year's holiday gifts. Start a list with the people you plan on purchasing gifts for. As you purchase the gifts write down who the gift is for, how much you paid for it, and where you purchased the gift. If you don't know what to buy as you're out for shopping, and you run across a sale look for things that you think they may like. If you have a copy machine, make a copy of the receipt, tape the receipt to the page in the notebook.

Homemade Cleaners

Ground-in-dirt

If wet, let dry, and then brush off as much as possible. Treat with a prewash stain remover (Spray'N Wash is a good one.) You can wait up to a week before laundering; with the spray versions it's best to wash immediately, before the liquid dries.

Grass Stains

Rub a liquid detergent that's enzyme-based into the stain. (Many major brands have an enzyme version; check the package.) Then wash using the hottest water recommended for the fabric. If it's safe to use chlorine bleach (read the care label), and add that as well.

Bird Droppings

Treat with a prewash stain remover or soak in warm water with a detergent containing enzymes, then launder. If the spot is still there, use an eyedropper to apply enough hydrogen peroxide to saturate the stain. Then apply a drop or two of unscented, suds-free ammonia. (Test the fabric first to make sure the dye doesn't run.) Rinse and launder again.

Pollen

Gently shake the garment to remove as many spores as possible. Then use the sticky side of a piece of tape to carefully lift off the remaining particles. Never brush off pollen with your hand. The oils from your skin may set the spot. Treat with a prewash stain remover, and launder. Check the label to see if you can use bleach.

Abrasive Cleaner

Mix vinegar and salt together for a good surface cleaner.

Linoleum and Vinyl Floor Cleaner

One cup of distilled white vinegar mixed into two gallons of water removes dull, greasy film on these types of floors.

Copper Cleaner

Mix a paste of lemon juice and salt, rub with a soft cloth, rinse with water and dry.

Ceramic Tile Cleaner

Mix one-fourth cup of vinegar into a gallon of hot water. You can add more vinegar if the tile is really dirty.

Stainless Steel Sink

To make the sink shine, rub with olive oil or lemon oil.

Appliance Cleaner

Lightly rub dry baking soda over the surface of the appliance. Wipe with a clean sponge and warm water.

Odors

White vinegar: Set out a few bowls, each containing half a cup of white vinegar and leave them overnight (where the kids and pets can't reach them). As the vinegar evaporates, the smell will vanish.

I know you're thinking that everything will smell like vinegar, vinegar (an acid) combines with the odor (typically alkaline), and the two neutralize each other—so you don't just replace fish stench with a vinegar one. If the smell is in the kitchen, you can do a quick fix by boiling three tablespoons of vinegar to one cup of water. (Keep an eye on the pan.)

Home Movies

How many times have you been looking for one of your home movies and had to look at this tape or that tape until you found it? It's very time consuming and sometimes frustrating. After the tape has been recorded, review the tape and write on the label what the tape contains along with the date. Label the tape and the tape case. Store by event or date for easy access.

Homework

The next time your child needs help with homework and you don't know what to do, try going to these Web sites.

- The Internet Public Library kidspace (www.ipl.org/div/kidspace): Does your child need an idea for the science fair? This site leads you to a link of projects as well as a homework help section.
- Fact Monster (www.factmonster.com): This site offers references to flash cards, multiplication tables, history timelines, and biographies of U.S. presidents.
- Kid Info (www.kidinfo.com): This site categorizes links according to the curriculum covered in most U.S. schools. You'll also discover online atlases, dictionaries, and encyclopedias.
- Math.com (www.math.com/parents/helpyourkids.htm): It takes you through the steps to finding a solution from basic addition to subtraction to ratios, algebra, and geometry.
- National Geographic Kids (www.kidsnationalgeographic.com): Takes a virtual tour of the natural world, including its people, places, flora, and fauna.
- BJ Pinchbecks Homework Helper (www.bjpinchbeck.com): This site offers over eight hundred updated links to subject matters from art to social studies . . . even recess. You'll also

find links to study guides, such as www.studygs.net that can help your child with time management and other learning skills.

Note: I have no financial or commercial interest in any Web sites, products, services, or professionals mentioned in this book.

Hosiery

If you're trying to put on pantyhose with rough hands, chances are you will get a run or sag in them before you get them on. To help with this, wash and dry your hands, then rub your hands with lotion; put your hose on while the lotion is still damp on your hands.

Hotlines

Sometimes no matter how much we try, our kids won't open up with us even when they're in serious trouble. Post this list where they can find it. It could be a lifesaver if your child has a friend that may need help, and they can pass it on to them. All lines are open twenty-four hours a day, seven days a week. They also take calls from worried parents.

Depression and suicide
The National Hopeline Network, 1-800-784-2433
Incoming calls get routed to a suicide crisis agency located near the caller. More than 40 percent of calls come from people between the age of fourteen and twenty-four.

Drug Abuse
U.S. Department of Health and Human Services, Substance Abuse Services Administration, 1-800-662-4357

Callers receive information on where to find treatment in their area for abuse of all types of substances, from alcohol to illegal (and legal) drugs.

Overdose
Poison Control Center, 1-800-222-1222

You may think of this as a number to call when someone accidentally swallows a substance like cleaning fluids. But Poison Control also takes calls concerning alcohol and drug abuse—many from teens worried that a friend has overdosed. Toxicologists are on hand to help the caller, figure out if he/she should take the friend to the emergency room or follow steps to deal with the problem on his/her own.

Runaways
National Runaway Switchboard, 1-800-786-2929

This hotline helps runaways find local shelters, transitional housing, and other resources. It can even arrange for them to get a free bus ticket home. Volunteers and professional staff also work to prevent troubled kids from leaving home in the first place.

Eating Disorders
National Eating Disorders Association, 1-800-931-2237

This helpline (staffed only during certain business hours) offers referrals to local support groups, treatment centers for anorexia, bulimia, and other eating problems. After-hour callers can leave a confidential voicemail: a staffer will call back promptly.

School Shootings
PAX Real Solutions to Gun Violence, 1-866-773-2587

In more than 80 percent of school-shooting cases, the attacker told at least one other student about his or her scheme beforehand. This is the number kids can call if they've heard about such plan. Callers are not required to reveal their identity. Trained counselors ask questions, and then call the school and local law enforcement to report the treat.

Any Issue
Girls and Boys Town National Hotline, 1-800-448-3000

This crisis, resource, and referral line is designed to help young people with problems ranging from fighting with parents, and bullying to sexual assault, and drug abuse.

Covenant House NINELINE, 1-800-999-9999

Staffers take calls on any subject and have access to a database of thirty thousand social service agencies throughout the country, including the fifteen Covenant House shelters.

Note: I have no financial or commercial interest in any Web sites, products, services, or professionals mentioned in this book.

Household Chores

Here is a way to get everyone in the house to pitch in with the household chores. Create a five-minute job jar; turn the mundane tasks into a game. Everyone can play. Make a list of all of the household chores that can be done in five minutes, ten minutes, fifteen minutes, and thirty minutes.

Be creative; use stock card in the different colors, add your own touch, make it fun, and get competitive. Get a timer, beat the clock, and get a free pass on the next challenge. Or whoever wins gets to pick the snacks for movie night or their favorite dinner. Another way to get everyone involved is a to-do list for each person: *your list, my list, and our list*. Every time you finish a project or chore, decide on a reward system. It could be something small each time something on the list is completed, or something big at the end.

Ice

Instead of throwing away the two-liter plastic soda bottles, recycle them by cutting the plastic bottle in half, and filling it halfway up with water and freezing it. After it has frozen, run water around the side of it and empty the ice into a container or ice pitcher for ice tea or ice water. The good thing is they are reusable and this will save you money.

Ice-cream Scoop

You can use the ice-cream scoop for more than just ice cream!

- The next time you make muffins instead of spooning the batter into the muffin cups, try using your ice-cream scoop. Scoop the batter, and just as you're filling the muffin cup, squeeze the handle to dispense the batter into the cup.
- When making pancakes try the scoop for the pancake batter. Works like a charm.
- The next time you're serving potato salad or slaw, use the ice-cream scoop. It's a perfect serving size, and it also has a nice presentation.
- The ice-cream scoop is great for portion control.

Iron Skillet

To season an iron skillet, coat lightly with cooking oil, put into the oven at three hundred degrees for thirty minutes. Let it cool. Note: Cook only cornbread or biscuits in your skillets. Always wipe the skillet with a paper towel when you're finished. Never soak in water or let water stay in the iron skillet. To clean, wash with dishwashing soap and water; do not put in the dishwasher. Reseason after every wash. But for daily use, just use a paper towel to clean up any excess.

Jeans/Clothes

Are you always getting the kid's jeans/clothes mixed up? A quick fix is to take a permanent marker and put one dot on the label of the first child's jeans/clothes, two dots for the second child's jeans/clothes, and so on. This works on hand-me-downs because you just add another dot as the jeans/clothes get passed down.

Jewelry

The next time you're at a flea market or a yard sale, look for some pretty drawer pulls. This is good for hanging necklaces. Mount the drawer pulls on the wall and hang the necklaces over it.

Jewelry Cleaner

Have you ever got ready to go out somewhere and were already dressed and ready to walk out of the door, when you noticed that your rings were dirty? Find a small spray bottle and label it jewelry cleaner. If in a hurry just spray a little on your rings, let it sit for a minute, rinse in warm water for a quick cleaning.

Junk Mail

Bubble Wrap and peanuts can be costly. A good way to recycle is to shred all junk mail. So the next time you need to mail something fragile, you'll have something to pack around the items. It's free and you've recycled. Did you know that anytime you enter a contest or order an item by mail, your name could end up on a mailing list that may be rented or sold to other companies?

To keep your information private, write "NO mailing list" beside your contact information, and always check the opting out of mailing list when you give your address online. Remove your name from any national mailing list by registering online at www.privateright.org (there is approximately a $1 charge) or send a signed, dated note with your name and address to:

Mail Preference Service
c/o Direct Marketing Association
PO Box 643 Carmel, NY 10512

For credit card offers call 1-888-5-OPT-OUT or 1-888-5-678-6881 a recorded message will prompt you to leave your name, address, telephone number, and social security number. Don't Worry they already have access to this information. For Junk e-mail protects your inbox by registering at www.privateright.org.

Note: I have no financial or commercial interest in any Web sites, products, services, or professionals mentioned in this book.

Karaoke Disc

To stop everyone from handling the CDs, design a CD holder by using a CD case that zips and holds one hundred or more disk. After every purchase of a CD, take a permanent marker and write the number on the CD disk starting your collection with disk #1 and so on. Make a binder with a list of every song on each disk. You can do this by song or by artist. After each entry of the song, type out beside it the CD disk number and the track number. Now no one is handling the CD disk. They are only looking at the binder that all the songs are in. Note: This works best if you have a computer, and do this in excel, and this way you can update as needed. For example:

Artist	Song	Disk	Track
Jane Doe	Any song	#1	12

Keepsake Items

When my daughter had our first grandchild, I gave her a beautiful wooden chest. She decided to dedicate that chest to her firstborn; first shoes, first blanket, first outfit, all the things you would want to give back to them when they get grown. I can't think of one gift that would be better to receive after you're grown than your own keepsakes.

Kids' Stuff

Kids have special spots at school. Why not at home for storing their books, sports gear, and jackets? Set up the same system at home by providing hooks and durable plastic tubs labeled with each child's name. When the kids get home after school, they should immediately hang their outerwear and put their things in their tub that's labeled with their name. Order labels from www. stuckonyou.biz or call 1-888-236-2800. They have vinyl name labels, clothing, and shoe labels.

Note: I have no financial or commercial interest in any Web sites, products, services, or professionals mentioned in this book.

Kitty Litter

Who said you had to have a cat to use kitty litter?

- The unscented kitty litter is a good way to eliminate damaging moisture. Put a handful in a sock (don't let it directly touch the stored items) and toss it in the corner of your closet or storage bins.
- Another good use is if you have a small gas or oil spill; use a cup or two to absorb the spill, discard following the EPA guidelines.
- Or make sachets stored with everything from clothes to tools.
- If you have a basement, set out a small bowl to help control moisture and dampness.

Keys

Keep extra set's of keys for everything.

- If you have two keys just alike, get them in different colors or shapes.
- Make master copies of all important keys, file them or put them in a safe.

- If you have someone you trust, give him or her a set in case of an emergency.
- In the wintertime I like to warm-up my car, especially on the very cold mornings. But I'm always afraid to leave my car running unattended and unlocked.
- I have two sets of keys to my car; the first set only has one key on the keyring, the second set of keys has my house key and car key on it. I crank my car with the set of keys that only has one key on the key ring, and I lock my car while it's warming. I use the second set to lockup my house, so if someone should decide to break the window; they are only getting one car key instead of the whole set.
- Before I enter my car, out of habit I always try to look at the backseat even if my car is locked.
- Upon entering my car, I always press the lock button, even though my car will lock when I put it into gear. I want the doors locked as soon as I get in there. I also think everyone should know if there is a safety feature that would allow you to open your trunk, just in case you're the victim. Keep one of your keyless remotes in the trunk if you can afford the extra one. This way you can get out if you need to. *You can never be too safe.*

Keyholes

Before cold weather strikes, dab a little petroleum jelly *on your keys, and move them* in and out of the keyhole of your house and cars.

Kitchen Cabinets

You would be surprised at how much space you can make by just being organized. Always place like-items with like-items. Have one cabinet for glasses; one cabinet for small, medium, and large bowls. If you have bowls with lids, place the lid upside down in your bowl. Now your bowls are stackable. Don't be afraid to stack always, making sure you stack the heaviest on the bottom. Have a cabinet just for plastic items such as bowls, lids, and plastic containers like tea pitchers. For everyday dishes place them in a cabinet that is large enough to hold the dinner plates, salad plates, cake plates, soup, and cereal bowls, cups, and saucers. Place them where they are functional. Store pots and pans the same way you would store your stackable bowls, turn the lids upside in the pan and stack them. Store all the baking pans, and cake pans together.

Kitchen Cabinet Knobs

If you are tired of the way your kitchen cabinetry looks, and you don't want the expense of purchasing new ones, try this. "Replace the knobs," sometimes just the little things make all the difference in the way some thing looks. Try looking at the flea market or an antique shop. Sometimes you can run across unique knobs there. You can also do the same thing with your restroom cabinetry.

Kitchen Drawers

Every kitchen needs these drawer's silverware, utensils, dishtowels, misc. items, and a tool drawer. Keep utensils that are used everyday in a decorative holder on the stove. If you don't have enough drawers, you could use decorative baskets for your dishtowels.

Turn the basket on it's side; roll up the towels and put them in the basket. This makes a nice decorative piece. This works very well in small spaces, especially if you're limited on drawer space.

Kitchen Sink

A good way to clean your kitchen sink without using strong abrasive chemicals is to take half a cup of table salt and half of a lemon; sprinkle the salt at the bottom of the sink, rub the lemon around in the salt, and then rinse with water. *Bar keepers friend* is also very good, and is great on copper.

Note: I have no financial or commercial interest in any Web sites, products, services, or professionals mentioned in this book.

Laundry

Why fight and dread it. It has to be done. I found what works for me. Before I go to sleep at night, I sort through that day's dirty clothes; most households have two loads a day. I put my colored clothes in the washer and fill the washer.

The next morning when I get up, I start the wash. After waking up and while I am drinking my coffee, the clothes are getting washed. Dry that load while you're getting ready for work or school, etc. If you don't have time to finish drying them, leave them in the dryer until you get home, finish drying them when you get back home. Always hang or fold your clothes while they are warm. This will reduce wrinkles.

Note: Never leave home with the washer and dryer running for safety reasons.

Laundry Room

Make your laundry room user-friendly. If you don't have enough storage space, put shelves over your washer and dryer. Find a place in your laundry room to hang up your clothes after they have finished drying; always dry your clothes for a few minutes, they hang better if they are warm. Store all of your detergent bleach and fabric softeners in your laundry room along with all of your paper products.

Leather

Never put away leather wet. Once with mildew, those items are ruined. Clean leather jackets, shoes, and purses with leather cleaners. Dry completely and apply leather dressing, a conditioner sold at most stores that carry leather goods.

Letters and Documents

Preserve precious love letters or newspaper clippings by photocopying them onto fine linen or cotton that hasn't been recycled. Rag paper, as it's also called, is much longer lasting than today's wood-pulp paper.

- Store documents unfolded in a dark place; remove paper clips or staples.
- Stack letters and photocopied clippings between pieces of acid-free paper in a tight-fitting storage box. Instead of folding large papers, roll them.

Life Story

There are as many ways to put together a family history as there are people to tell the stories. Create a simple written document illustrated with photos. Tell the story of many generations, focus on just one person or create a snapshot of a historical moment. It can also include contributions from family members in the form of letters or narratives of their life experiences. Talk to your elders; don't wait until it's too late, because when they're gone there's no getting them back.

Lightbulbs

Replacing regular inefficient light bulbs with compact fluorescent Light bulbs (CFLs) can make a difference. A CFL is 70 to 75 percent more efficient than other bulbs. The cost will be a little more than the regular bulbs, but you should save money on your electricity bill overtime. Three bulbs can last for approximately eight to ten years. If every family replaces one bulb with a CFL, it would be like reducing carbon emissions from eight hundred thousand cars. The new and improved light bulbs cost approximately six dollars, and they give off a beautiful light, and they also can be adapted to dimmers. If you can't afford to purchase all the bulbs at one time, purchase one or two every time you purchase your groceries.

Note: I have no financial or commercial interest in any Web sites, products, services, or professionals mentioned in this book.

Lingo

Internet Acronyms Parents Need to Know:
If you have teenagers that are on the computer or texting, here is a Web site that can help you figure out the lingo. Go to www. netlingo.com for a list of the acronyms and expressions used. Here is a sample of what you will find.

- PIR: Parent in room
- POS: Parent over shoulder
- ASL: Age, sex, location
- LMIRL: Let's meet in real life
- ADR: Address
- WYCM: Will you call me
- BRB: Be right back
- C-P: Sleepy

This is just a sample. Every parent should know about the lingo. It's scary in today's society with all of the child predators out there that are just waiting to prey on our children and teens. Also if your teen has a MySpace, twitter, or facebook page, join whatever social networking site your teen uses and become one of his or her "friends." This will give you access to your teen's social network where you can get to know your teen's peers.

There is also another site (www.wiredwithwisdom.org): This is a site that lets your teen virtually experience tracking an online sex predator. This game is used in law enforcement and classes. Other online resources (www.benetsafe.com): If you're worried that your teen may have several social networking pages, and you don't have time to monitor your teen on a regular basis, this service will monitor for a fee and notify you by e-mail if he or she gives out personal information or participation in dangerous practices. There are Christian alternatives to MySpace, twitter, and facebook, that promote online social networking among Christians www.mypraize.com.

Note: I have no financial or commercial interest in any Web sites, products, services, or professionals mentioned in this book.

Loose Change

Loose change always comes in handy; you would be surprised how this can add up. At the end of the year, if you have not saved enough, add some to it, purchase an IRA, or put it toward something you have been wanting. Or just save it for an emergency. Drop your loose change in a decorative jar and forget about it.

Lotion

Purchase a large bottle of lotion and small bottle of lotion. When the small bottle runs out or runs low, simply refill it with the large bottle of lotion. Use the pump nozzle on the large bottle of lotion to refill the small bottle. Refill by pumping it in. Keep the small bottle in your purse.

Magazines

Every time I go to the grocery store, I can't help but buy a magazine. I would read it and then throw it away or let them stack up just taking up space. So now I save mine, if you have this problem donate them to a nursing home, doctor's office, or shelter. Anywhere they could be put to use. Or you could take them to work and swap out the ones you've read for the ones you haven't read with your coworkers.

Note: If you receive them through the mail take a permanent marker, and mark out your name or peel off the label. For magazines that you want to keep and read later, carve out a private corner in an open room by placing a shuttered divider next to your favorite chair. The slats give you space to store dozens of newspapers and magazines in plain view. To make a screen; take three old shutters, connect them with hinges, for a finishing touch clip on a lamp and drape a soft throw over the chair.

Magnets

The next time you have to climb a ladder and hold onto your nails or screws, put a magnet on the ladder. This will hold them in place. You can buy the thin flat one's and glue them to the back of a notepad, and then you can put it on the refrigerator.

Mail

It's so easy to let the mail stack up and clutter up the tables and the counters. After a while you feel like you're drowning in junk mail and bills. I found that if everyday after I retrieve the mail from the mailbox, if I open it right then and either keep it, throw it away or shred it, then it's not so bad. After I open the mail, I file it in the letter rack and I throw away or shred the junk mail.

To remove your name from many of the national mailing lists by registering with the direct *Marketing Association's Mail Preference Service*. Register online at www.privateright.org offmailinglist

(There is approximately a $1 charge) or send a signed, dated note with your name and address too.

Mail Preference Service
c\o Direct Marketing Association
PO Box 643
Carmel, NY 10512

Note: I have no financial or commercial interest in any Web sites, products, services, or professionals mentioned in this book.

Mascara

The next time your mascara brush gets caked up with dried-up mascara, take a cotton ball and dip it in eye makeup remover and wipe the brush wand and around the rim of the mascara. This will keep your mascara from getting on all of your other makeup. You can also use the remover to get the excess makeup out of your makeup bag.

Making the Most of Your Food Dollar

Today's families are faced with more demands than ever. Time and money are two resources that no one ever seems to have enough of, so it's important to make the most of them. There are a few simple things you can do to stretch the food dollar.

- Preplanning saves food dollars. Try to plan meals for one week in advance.
- Stock up on items that are on sale and those that have an extended shelf life. Avoid spending money on sale items if they are not in your weekly meal plan.

- Use coupons, whenever possible you can find them on the Internet, through your local newspaper, and your local grocery store.
- Generic or store brands are good choices too, because they usually cost less and have the same nutritional value as brand name items.
- Try "batch cooking" when time allows. Cooking large batches of main dishes, casseroles, etc. can save you time and money if you utilize the leftovers for meals to take to work, school, etc.
- Avoid convenience food when possible. Not only are they more expensive, but also they are high in sodium, fat, and sugar.
- Eat a healthy breakfast! It still is the most important meal of the day, and it will keep you from snacking all day long.
- There are a variety of programs available to help families with food needs. Contact your county extension office, social services, clergy, or the local food bank for more information on programs that may be available to help you.
- Build family time into mealtime. Try to eat meals together as a family. This will help encourage open communication and reduce stress.

Meat

The next time you go grocery shopping and you purchase meat, save time by marinating it first. Put the meat with all your seasoning in a zip-top freezer bag and freeze. Don't forget to put the date on it. When you're ready to use it, the work is already done. Remove from the freezer; let it thaw in the refrigerator overnight, the meat marinates as it thaws.

Medicine

A good way to keep track of all of your medication is to keep it all in one place. For the medications that you take everyday, purchase a seven-day organizer holder. Measure out the doses for each day. This will also help you to remember if you took your medicine for that day. If you don't have a seven-day organizer, you can turn the bottle upside down after you have taken it for the day; I do this sometimes. Also remember to keep all medications out of reach of children. Keep all over-the-counter medications separated from the prescription medications.

Another good thing to do is always keep a list with everyone in the home that is taking medication. The list should include who is taking it, for what condition, and the prescribing doctor. Also check the expiration dates. Keep a list in your wallet, purse, or handbag; just in case of an accident as well as the name of an emergency contact person.

Medical History

At some point in your life, you may need your medical records. It is a good idea to collect your medical records from all of the doctors you've ever been to. This is really a good idea for new mothers with newborns, because you're taking charge now. I just recently put mine together. The way I put my medical records together was, I started contacting all of the doctors that I had gone to in the past and present. I went back fifteen years. I contacted each one and did what I could over the phone. I then went to their office and signed the release forms for my medical files. Sometimes they will charge a fee per copy; pay it, you will be glad you did. After I finished gathering all of my medical information, I purchased a three-ring binder and I started putting everything in that binder by date order.

Also if you have a medical condition and you don't have insurance, you may be able to get free medical attention by going to www. clinicaltrials.gov or ask your doctor to call 1-800-411-1222 to find out if your condition is currently being studied. If you are uninsured, you can pay approximately $7.95 and you can get a medical cost report from www.healthgrades.com Click on health manager to find the going rate in your area for more than fifty different procedures.

Note: I have no financial or commercial interest in any Web sites, products, services, or professionals mentioned in this book.

Message Board

Turn a cabinet into a message board by brushing on chalkboard paint. Apply two coats right over the existing finish, let dry, and now you're ready to start jotting down you're grocery list or reminders. Try this on a lower door as a drawing spot for the kids. Another good way would be to find a frame in the style that you like. Paint the backing with the chalkboard paint. Add the backing to the frame; place the framed work on the wall.

Memory Clutter

If you've ever lost someone near and dear to you as I have, it is hard to let go of his or her belongings. If you have the space that is good, but if you're limited on space keep a few items. Keep the items that truly mean something to you. Sort everything into three categories: charity, donations, and keepsakes. You can incorporate your loved one's belongings by placing in your loved one's belongings with yours.

Muffin Pans

Making tacos can be very messy when you don't have a taco holder for the shells. A good way to stand the shells up, to fill them, is to turn the muffin pan upside down, slide the shell into the space, then fill. Also another good use for the muffin pan is to bake your stuffing, which would make a beautiful display for the holiday table.

Nails

Have you ever been trying to work with a nail that was so small you could barley hold it? A quick fix for this is to use a comb, put the nail between the teeth to hold it; this will keep it steady and keeps your fingers from getting smashed with the hammer.

Name Labels

To cut down on your child losing his/her clothes while away from home, such as camp or school, put their names on their clothes. Go to www.namelabels.com or call 1-866-952-2357. These labels are very inexpensive, and will help to keep you from (A) replacing clothes unnecessarily and (B) help you in sorting the laundry. Also if you have someone in a nursing home, this is a requirement.

Note: I have no financial or commercial interest in any Web sites, products, services, or professionals mentioned in this book.

Networking

If you are a business owner, here are some ideas that might help you prosper and save you money, all at the same time.

- Join your local Chamber of Commerce; there is a small membership fee, and they will promote your business.
- Get with the other business's in your area, and network exchange business cards.
- Hold networking functions at your place of business; this will draw potential customers inside your business.
- Twitter, Facebook and MySpace.com is great, because you can network and there is no charge. It's free advertisement. Link your site to anyone who will let you, and do the same for other businesses.
- Make business cards; this is good for small businesses. Attach that card to your merchandise with a pretty ribbon; packaging is everything.
- Also use both sides of the card, the more information you can put on it the better. On one side put the business information, on the other side put pictures. Design something unique and different; set yourself apart from everyone else. Have a unique quote!
- Offer free gift wrapping; customers love that added touch.
- People are looking for a unique experience.
- Have a guest register, have all your customers sign it with their name, address, and e-mail address, so you can send them a note when you're having a special sale or event.

Newspaper Clippings

Newspaper clippings or articles are easily lost or misplaced. Make a scrapbook for these clippings. Section it off for the different events such as birth announcements, death notices, athletic events, or for clippings you would like to refer back to. If there is a subject that you have more clippings of, make a scrapbook on just that subject. Get a Ziploc baggie or a file folder, label the file and newspaper clippings, file them, and save this task for a rainy day.

No Gloves

If ever you're in a situation that you need gloves to clean something or pick up something, and you don't have a pair, a quick fix for this is to use a plastic bag, slip it over your hand, and wrap it around so it's secure. If you don't have either of the two, do it later.

Outside Shower

If you do a lot of yard work, think about this. Install an outside shower. This will keep you cool in the summertime heat. I do a lot of yard work in the summertime; I will, on the really hot days, get under the shower to get cooled off. Before we installed the outside shower, I would always get under the water hose; I was always tracking in grass and dust throughout the house. I set up a station with towels and extra changes of clothes in the garage, so after I rinse off, I dry off and change my wet clothes. You are probably thinking why you would want to get wet in your clothes. The answer is simple: On the really hot days you'll do anything to stay cool, including stepping under an outside shower, and the kids love it.

Packing to Move

A good way to stay organized is to think ahead.

Gather all of your supplies.

- Boxes
- Rubbermaid containers with lids for fragile items. (Clear Rubbermaid's)
- Tape gun and tape.
- Permanent colored markers.
- Bubble Wrap: You can purchase Bubble Wrap packing material in various widths and in large and small textures. It's reusable.
- Packing and tissue paper: You can purchase tarnish-free paper for silver, and acid-free paper for linens.
- Blankets: Heavy and light.
- Plywood is good for securing mirrors, painting, and artwork. Cut it to fit each mirror. Staple Bubble Wrap to the piece of plywood to give it cushion, and lay the piece you're moving on top of the plywood.
- Envelopes or Ziploc baggies: To keep screws, keys, and any hardware that might otherwise get misplaced; label the front of the envelope and tape it to the furniture or pack in the box or container.
- Last but not the least, assign a different color marker to each room. Mark each box or container with the permanent marker that you've assigned for that room. *For example, yellow for the kitchen.* As you move the boxes, place them in the room they belong to. This will keep you from moving the boxes multiple times.

Paint

Got leftover paint from your last project? Instead of storing an entire gallon can of paint for only a few cups of paint, pour the remaining paint into a smaller airtight aluminum or plastic container. Label the outside with a paint smudge and any important information, so you'll know which can to grab when it's time for touch ups. Baby jars are perfect for this.

Painting

The next time you open a fresh can of paint, try this tip. Slide a rubber band over the top of the paint can, then gently wipe the bottom of the brush against the rubber band, each time you dip. This is perfect for small containers without handles. The brush will be less drippy, and the can's rim will stay clean, making it easier when putting the lid on when you're finished.

Paint Colors

You want to repaint your home, but you can't remember what color you used before. This happens especially when you have the colors mixed. Make a file just for that. Keep the labels from the paint can along with the sample color, formula, and the brand of paint that was used; don't forget where you purchased your paint from. Keep the receipt or just make a note for the file.

Paint Rollers

If you have to paint around your home, and you know it will take a couple of days to finish, this is a way to store the paint rollers. After you have finished painting for the day, put the paint roller in a small trash bag and wrap it properly, so no air can get into it. Then place it in the freezer until the next day. Take it out an hour before you're ready to use it. It works very well; now you're not out to the expense of purchasing another roller.

Paint Tray

The next time you paint, try this; cover the paint tray with an aluminum foil, and then pour your paint in the tray. When you've finished painting, throw away the aluminum foil, and the pan is already clean or just purchase a liner for the pan.

Pantry

Do you get tired of every time you need something from the pantry; you find yourself moving everything in the pantry in order to get to that one item you were looking for? Keep your can goods in order by vegetable with the labels facing out, so when you open the pantry you can see everything. This will also help you take an inventory at a glance. So you don't duplicate items that you already have.

However, I do like to keep at least two of everything that I use daily, such as coffee, tea, sugar, and creamer. I like to keep all of my packaged rice, sauces, and mixes in a Tupperware container. All of my cooking spices, I will keep on a Lazy Susan. I also have a cabinet that is used for extra spices; spices are very expensive;

I try to buy them throughout the year when I can catch them on sale. Now I am prepared for the holidays.

Note: To check the expiration date on your spices, you can go to www.spicecheckchallenge.com and enter the code on the bottom of your McCormick jar, and find out if it is still in date.

Note: I have no financial or commercial interest in any Web sites, products, services, or professionals mentioned in this book.

Paper Cups

Are you always the one who opens the cabinet and you find that there are no glasses because they're dirty in the sink or dishwasher? This usually happens because everyone thinks that every time they need something to drink; they have to get a clean glass, instead of reusing the glass they started out with. My fix for this is to get the 16oz paper or foam cups for hot and cold drinks, write their names on the cup. They don't sweat and are reusable.

Party Planning

The next time you're planning a party, enlist anyone who wants to be a part of the excitement and expense. If you don't want to have the party at your house, find a place that you can rent out for an evening. Everyone can share the expense on the rent, food, and entertainment; this should take the burden off of the one person.

Peroxide

Peroxide has many uses besides cleansing wounds. It is inexpensive and has very little odor.

- Let your toothbrush soak in a cup of peroxide to keep them germfree.
- Clean your counters and tabletops with peroxide to kill germs, this leaves a fresh smell. Simply put a little on your dishrag when you wipe or spray it on the counters.
- After rinsing off your cutting board, pour peroxide on it to kill any bacteria such as salmonella.
- Fill a spray bottle with 50/50 mixture of water and peroxide, and keep it in the bathroom to disinfect without harming your septic system.
- You can also add a cup of peroxide to your white clothes instead of bleach. If there is blood on the clothing, pour it directly on the soiled spot, let it sit for a minute, and then rub it and rinse with cold water. Repeat as necessary. Note: Hot water will set in a bloodstain, always use cold water.
- You can also use peroxide to clean your mirrors, there is no smearing. Put some peroxide in a spray bottle spray it on and wipe off.

Picnic Basket

Use a picnic basket that has a lid and no one will know what's in there. Store things that you use when you're doing your yard work such as first-aid kit, work gloves, protective eyewear, sunglasses, fanny packs, sun-visors, or hats. This way it's right there and you won't waste time gathering up these things before you start your yard work.

Pictures

There are many different styles of the decorative photo boxes. Look for the ones that have the dividers in them. You can separate your pictures by events or holidays. You can set it up so that you have separated all birthdays, Christmas's, Thanksgiving's, family reunions, and graduations.

Find the decorative photo boxes that fit the occasion. When possible, store your pictures electronically. Scan the originals and store the originals in a safe place for safekeeping. By scanning your pictures, you can put them on a disk. It's also smart to make extra copies of photos, and give other family members copies just in case a disaster strikes.

Picture Frames

A neat way to personalize picture frames. Keep all of your old picture frames. You can purchase the letters at your local craft store. Paint them the color you want them, and then glue them in place. If you're not one that cares for the personalized frames, you could add butterfly, birds, flowers, or jewels to them. They make great gifts.

Pillows

Everyone has a certain pillow that they sleep on, but if you have the same pillowcase on each pillow, how can you tell your pillow from your spouse's pillow? A quick fix for this is to tie a ribbon and pin it at the end of your pillowcase or use pillowcases of a different color. Find a button that would complement the pillowcase and sew a button at the end of the pillowcase. So you can tell your pillow from your spouse's.

Pet Supplies

Keep pet supplies together such as medicines, shampoos, brushes, collars, and sweaters. This helps in keeping track of what's on hand. Keep all supplies separated by animal since all their needs are different.

Pens, Pencils, and Markers

Use clear containers with lids for easy access. Separate all pens, pencils, and markers. Keep each of them in their own container; label each container of the contents. If you don't have clear containers use Ziploc baggies.

Place Markers

After your next dinner party, save the stoppers of the bottles. Bundle six together, and they become an anchor for a decorative place cardholder. Tie the six corks together with twine, ribbon, or raffia (secure with glue if needed); then use card stock paper with your guest name's written on it. Calligraphy pens have such an elegant style.

Place Mats

Store place mats from a hook or office clip. This will help keep them from wrinkling, hang them inside your pantry on the inside door.

Plastic Containers

Coat your plastic container with a nonstick spray before adding a tomato-based sauce. This will help to keep the plastic from turning orange and staining it.

Potluck

- Potluck means less cooking for the host. It requires some planning. Assign food categories to your guest or ask them to bring a specific dish, such as potato salad or slaw. If some guest prefers not to cook, they can supply beverages, plates, or utensils.
- Strategize with your guest to avoid last minute chaos in the kitchen. Ask your guest if their dish will be finished when they arrive or whether they will need additional cooking time.
- If you're attending a potluck, try making a dish that's easy to transport and that only needs last-minute heating.
- The casserole has become a staple potluck since it travels so well. Transport your dish by placing something under it to keep it from sliding around.
- Dishes served at room temperature, such as pasta or chopped salads, are ideal for parties.
- Last but not the least, label your serving dishes with address labels. To remove it just peel it off. This will take all the guesswork out of who has what serving dish.
- I purchase my labels from www.ipclabels.com/reorder or mail approximately $6.95 for 500 labels to: Labels PO Box 3200 Salem, VA 24153 Note: Prices may be subject to change.

Note: I have no financial or commercial interest in any Web sites, products, services, or professionals mentioned in this book.

Power Strip

Most people don't know that plugged-in appliances and electronic devices use energy even if they're turned off. We're spending all this money to power things that are in the off position. To cut your electricity cost, plug in your electronic devices to the smart power strip, which retails for approximately $32.95. When you turn off the power strip, all items plugged into it will also power down. Over time you should see your monthly electricity bill and your energy usage decrease. If you cannot purchase all of the strips that you need to cover each room, purchase them one at a time, until you get them all. You'll be glad you did. Not only are you saving money, but you're protecting your appliances too.

Note: I have no financial or commercial interest in any Web sites, products, services, or professionals mentioned in this book.

Proof of Valuables for Insurance Purposes

One good way to prove to the insurance company that you had the items you said that you had, would be to record these items with your camcorder.

- The first option would be to record each room of your home and name each item along with the serial number. Label the tape and put it in a safe place such as your homeowner's insurance file or safe for future reference.
- The second option would be to take pictures of each item. On the back of the picture, write the serial number and other pertinent information. Make a binder. Tape the picture to a piece of paper and put it in a sheet protector.
- The third option is to use your digital camera and store the memory card along with your insurance papers. Note: Some

insurance companies may require receipts. You could also make copies for all of your big ticket items and add to your binder or file as well.

- The forth option would be on your computer. Go to www. knowyourstuff.org and download the file, save the complete report on your computer. File a hard copy in your safe or safe deposit box at the bank.

Note: I have no financial or commercial interest in any Web sites, products, services, or professionals mentioned in this book.

Quick Fixes

Clogged spray bottles: Hold the nozzle under running hot water, then remove the residue with a tissue or use a toothpick to gently scrap away any debris logged in the hole.

Bottle cap on nail polish: Run hot water over the bottle to loosen the dried nail polish stuck around the rim. The next time you do your nails, wipe the rim of the bottle with nail polish remover. Another good fix for this is a rubber jar opener. It is slip resistant and will grab hold of the bottle cap.

Felt-tip markers: To remove stains from hands, wipe off with a cotton ball soaked in rubbing alcohol.

Sliding doors: Rub the track with a little floor polish, and then move the door back and forth along the track.

Bed slats: Put rubber bands over the end of the slats. This will keep them in place. Grip – it Shelve liners have a rubber texture they are slip resistant. Cut a piece to fit the board. Glue it to the back.

Potluck: The next time you have to take something for pot luck dinner; to keep from spilling it before you get there, place what you have cooked on top of the Grip-it rubber shelve liner (purchase at Wal-mart) in the back of your car. This will keep your dinner from sliding all over the place.

Pencils and pens: Put a rubber band around the end of the pencil or pen. This will keep it from rolling. Add a flower by taping it to the end of your pencil or pen. This will keep anyone from lifting it.

Sticky iron: Starch buildup or residue from synthetic fabrics burnt by high heat can coat an iron and keep it from gliding easily. Apply a hot iron cleaner like Dritz. Iron off.

Tree sap on deck: Soak a clean cloth with mineral spirits and carefully rub the spot (do a spot test first). Rinse thoroughly.

Weeds: To kill weeds in the walkway or in the cracks that poke through in a patio or sidewalk, try spraying the leaves and crowns with white vinegar or roundup.

Quart-size Baggies: When making deviled eggs instead of spooning in the filling, fill the bag with the filling for the deviled eggs. Cut a small hole in the bottom corner after you fill it up. Squeeze the filling into the egg.

Soap: To preserve the life of your soap and create a chic look at the same time, scatter a single layer of rocks of your choice on a dish and place the wet bar of soap on the top. The elevated groves allow the suds and water to drain away quickly.

Scissors: When scissors keep getting rusty, rub them with fine steel wool. Don't rub the blade. Wipe off any residue with a clean cloth. Spray the scissors with lubricating oil like WD-40. Then open and close.

Scorched pan: Fill a pan with two cups of water. Let the water come to a boil on the stove. Let it cool. Wash with dish soap.

Recipe cards: Keep your recipe cards clean by elevating them. Thread the card through the tines of a dinner fork. Then, stand it in a glass.

Rugs: To keep the edges from curling up on your rug, cover the area with a damp pressing cloth and iron the edges on both sides. Repeat until it lies flat.

Return address labels: Make sure your favorite serving dish is returned. Put one of your address labels on the serving pieces. The labels also peel off easily for washing.

Balsamic Vinegar: Add a few drops to the water when boiling eggs. The balsamic vinegar will slightly tint the eggs so you can tell the raw ones from the cooked ones; this also helps in preventing them from cracking.

Baked on cooking spray: Nonstick cooking spray leaves a residue if the dish isn't cleaned thoroughly. To remove the stubborn stain buildup on glass, *bar keepers friend* is great. It is a cleaner and polish with mild abrasives. It is great on stainless steel, copper, porcelain, etc.

Reading Glasses

If you are always misplacing your reading glasses, then this is for you. Keep extra pairs of glasses in hand in different parts of your home: in the restroom, kitchen, den in your purse, and in your car. You can purchase inexpensive reading glasses at the drug store.

Recipes for Household Cleaners

These mix-it self-cleaners are environmentally safe. If you're not sure it's right for the surface, test it on a small area first.

Glass Cleaner
Two cups water
Half cup white or cider vinegar
One-fourth cup rubbing alcohol
(70 percent concentration)

Glass Cleaner
One to two drops of scented oil such as orange essential oil, which gives the solution a great smell (optional) is great for windows and mirrors.

Combine and store ingredients in a spray bottle. Hint: Don't clean windows on a hot and sunny day, because the solution will dry too quickly and leave streaks.

Heavy-duty Scrub
Half a lemon
Half cup borax (a laundry booster)
Great for: rust stains on porcelain or enamel sinks and tubs.
Dip the lemon into borax and scrub the surface and rinse (Not safe on marble).

Grease Cleaner
Mix half cup of sudsy ammonia with enough water to fill a one-gallon container. (Sudsy ammonia which has detergent in it helps remove the tough grime.)

Great for: Oven hoods, grills

Dip the sponge in the solution. Wipe over the surface, and then rinse the area with clear water.

All-purpose Cleaner and Deodorizer
- Four tablespoons baking soda
- One quarter warm water

Great for kitchen counters, appliances, and inside the refrigerator.

Pour solution on a clean sponge and wipe then rinse area with warm water.

Lemon Juice
Great for fading stains on unfinished wood, such as a butcher block.

Apply full strength with a cotton ball, and then let it air-dry.

Cream of Tartar

Great for removing rust from white porcelain fixtures:

- Mix two tablespoons of cream of tartar with a few drops of 3 percent hydrogen peroxide to make a paste. Apply to the stain and let it sit. After the paste dries, rinse off.

Cornstarch

Great for absorbing oil and grease spills on clothing, upholstery, and leather.

Pat on enough corn starch to cover the stains (try to get them before they set); let it set awhile, then remove with a toothbrush or vacuum.

Refrigerator

Do you get tired when every time you need something out of the refrigerator, you have to move everything in there to get to one item? Put a lazy Suzanne in there. Store items such as mustard, mayo, and ketchup on it. This way you can spin it around to get what you are looking for.

Reflective Vest

Driving at night can be dangerous, but breaking down can be deadly especially if you have to get out and walk on a highway. Keep a reflective vest in your vehicle so you can be seen.

Rent It

You can save big by renting items online. Rentals let you test big-ticket purchases. If you're looking for an evening gown by designers like Versace, go to www.onenightaffair.com or call 310-474-7808 with your height, heel height, bust, waist, and hip measurements. So now you have a gown now you need a handbag at www.bagborroworsteal.com there is a monthly membership fee from approximately $5 to $9.95 a month, then you're charged for renting particular items at one of four increasingly expensive levels. Even on less costly levels you can find great stuff. Don't forget the jewelry at www.borrowedbling.com charges a monthly membership fee starting at approximately $29, which lets you rent up to two items at a time. www.Bagborroworsteal.com also stocks a range of designer precious and semiprecious pieces in sterling, gold, and white gold. Weekly jewelry rentals starting at approximately $8 (plus the monthly membership fee of approximately $5 to $9.95 other designers include Channel,Gucci, and Vera Wang. You can even rent furniture go to www.furniturerent.com

Note: Be sure to read the site's damage and thief policies before renting anything. Also print out a copy to refer back to.

Note: I have no financial or commercial interest in any Web sites, products, services, or professionals mentioned in this book.

Ride to School

If you have kids that are always fussing over who gets to ride in the front seat, a good solution is to make the child or teen that rides in the front on the way to school, ride in the back on the way home. Plus he or she has to take the first bath in the evening.

Salad Spinner

To preserve lettuce, get a salad spinner. You can purchase them at Wal-mart for approximately $2.98. Not only does it make washing the lettuce easy, it will preserve it longer. Just chop up the lettuce and put it in the salad spinner. Run water through it and the spinner takes all the excess water off the lettuce.

Note: I have no financial or commercial interest in any Web sites, products, services, or professionals mentioned in this book.

Sales Rack

When shopping, I am always looking to find a deal. So the first rack or section I go to is the sales rack. I always look for that unique and different item. I look for items that I can redecorate with that way I can change things up throughout the year. I always look for Christmas and Thanksgiving decorations such as, centerpieces and table linens. I like to Christmas shop throughout the year; so when the holidays are upon me, I'm not in a financial strain, and I can still make my monthly bills.

Each time I buy a gift, I write it down in my notebook. I write down the item, the amount, the name of the person the gift is going to, and where I purchased it. I never purchase a gift that

I wouldn't want for myself. I also wrap the gifts I purchase as I go, so that part is behind me and I don't have to worry about anyone seeing his or her gift. I also have a tradition every year the day after Thanksgiving. I put my Christmas tree up my gifts are wrapped and under the tree that night.

Sandpaper

If you are a crafty person and you work with a variety of sandpapers, you need a system. File the sheets ahead of time. Label each one with the grit numbers in an expandable file folder. Each time you buy a new grit, label it and file it.

Sandwiches

On those occasions when you have a get-together or gathering and you're in charge of the sandwiches, a quick fix for preparing them and keeping them fresh and from getting dry and stale, is to fix the sandwiches ahead of time. Cut them and place them on the tray that they are to be served on. Get a paper towel wet with water. Wring out the excess water and drape it over the sandwiches. Refrigerate sandwiches until you're ready to serve them. No one will ever know that you didn't just make them.

Scarfs, Ties, and Belts

Buy the regular belt, tie, and scarf hangers that hang in the closet. A shoe caddie works well. Instead of shoes, roll your ties and belts up and store them where you can see them clearly and have easy access.

Seasonal Clothes

Every year I pack up my winter clothes and pull out my summer clothes. I always pack my winter and summer clothes in the clear Rubbermaid's. They are airtight, durable, and stackable. If you don't have space to use the Rubbermaid's, you could use the Rubbermaid's that slide under the bed. I always keep the bags that have the zippers on them. No matter what the size, you would be amazed at what you can store in them.

Seasonal Cleaning

- Start with the mattress. Strip all the beds. Vacuum the surface and flip over. Vacuum under the bed. Dust off anything that is stored under there. Wash the mattress pad in the hottest water possible for the fabric.
- Clean the draperies at least once a year. If care instructions allow, machine-wash and hang to dry. At the very least, dust them off with the vacuum's upholstery attachment. Air the draperies on the clothesline occasionally to refresh them between cleaning or tumble them in the dryer on air-fluff without a heat setting.
- Vacuum blinds with the brush attachment. Close the blind and then reverse adjustable slats so you can get to both sides. If the blinds are stained and really dirty, just vacuuming them won't do it. Remove them from the window and soak them in the bathtub. Add half a cup of bleach to hot water. Let them soak. Then rinse the blinds. Let them air-dry. They should be clean and back white. Wooden blinds should be wiped off with a damp cloth slat by slat.
- Vacuum and dust the neglected areas of the refrigerator. Remove the grill and vacuum the refrigerator coil. Also check

the drip pan on your refrigerator. If you ever have an odor and you don't know where it's coming from, check that. Chances are you'll be right. It will smell like sour milk. Vacuum all baseboards, vacuum all areas not normally vacuumed through out the year.

- Wash all collectables. If your collectables can't be washed, dust them off.

Security Systems with Recorders

For security system that requires changing the tape everyday, finding a place to store the tapes can create a problem if you don't have a large space. I found that the canvas shoe bags hanging over the door works well. Labeled each tape 1-31 two tapes will fit into each pocket. This will hold a one-month supply. This really works for small space. The canvas shoe bag could be used for a lot of different things such as the bathroom for cosmetics, art supplies just hang it over the door label the pouches the possibilities are endless.

Sewing Kit

Every now and then I need a needle and thread even though I don't sew, but I sometimes have to. A sewing basket is great for the experienced seamstress. But for the inexperienced, a small decorative box will do just fine. I found a small decorative box, and I put the basic needs in there: needles, tread, scissors, tape measure, and safety pins.

Shampoo

I love to try the new shampoos that come out. I always have a little left over. Instead of throwing it out, I use it to refill my hand soap bottles. If you have more than one brand, mix them together. Discard the shampoo bottle. Now you just saved your self some money and cleaned out a cabinet.

Sheer Panel or Curtains

Have you ever washed your sheer panels and dried them? Have you discovered they were more wrinkled when you took them out of the dryer, than they were before you put them in to dry? If you wash them and then dry them for about three minutes and hang them while they are still very damp, this will pull most of the wrinkles out.

Sheets

There is nothing better than taking a nice hot bath and slipping into a freshly made bed with crisp clean sheets. This is one of life's simple pleasures. One big mistake that can be made when purchasing sheets is relying solely on the thread count. The thread count only tells half the story! Here's what to consider when shopping for sheets:

- Don't put too much stock in the label. Only buy sheets you can actually feel. Ask the sales clerk to open the package so you can touch them.
- Thread count is the number of threads per square inch. Most sheets are between 180 and 300 thread count. A higher thread count may mean a softer sheet, but this isn't always the case. The type of cotton used and weave also comes into play.

- Egyptian cotton is considered one of the best. It has longer threads that create a smoother, softer weave. But make sure that it's a long staple yarn that has been combed, woven in Italy, and has high thread count.
- A cotton-polyester blend isn't as soft as pure cotton but is easier to care for and doesn't wrinkle as much.
- Sateen is very luxurious. It is 100 percent cotton that's woven to have a slight sheen. (Don't confuse this with satin, which is a shiny polyester fabric.) Sateen bedding is delicate. So be sure to care for it properly.
- Linen and silk are great. If you live in a hot climate, these sheets will last for decades but they do require special care. Linen sheets will also need to be ironed, unless you like the shabby, chic look. Sheets and bedding always go on sale. So don't pay full price.
- I used to always misplace the pillowcases to my sheet sets, until I started folding my pillowcases together as one. Then I would place them in the center of my flat sheet. Once you finish folding them, they are all together. You can also fold the set of sheets and then place them inside one of the pillowcases.

Shoes

There's no such thing as "too many shoes" if they're organized and in good shape. One can divide the shoes into three categories: off-season, special occasion, and everyday wear. Store off-season shoes in a flat storage bin under your bed or in the clear shoe boxes at the bottom of your closet. Store special occasion shoes in the original box at the bottom of the closet. Store everyday shoes in an over-the-door shoe rack.

Another way would be to take pictures and tape the pictures to the end of the box. It's whatever works for you and how much detail you want to put into the project. The best time to purchase shoes is when the new season is coming in such as the spring. Then you can purchase the winter shoes cheaper, because they are being cleared out.

Shoe Caddie

Get creative in the way you store things such as cosmetics, office supplies, crafting projects, tools, hats, and gloves. The list could go on and on. Look for the shoe caddies that hang over the door. There are different styles such as vinyl and cloth. Who says that they have to be used for shoes?

Shovels

Never put your shovels away as they are expensive. If you have to replace them, so after every use, wash all the dirt off them. This will help to keep them from rusting. After every use always put the tools away. Never leave tools out in the weather. Spray them with W-40 and wipe them off. If your shovels are already rusted, you can purchase at the hardware store, a product called Navel Jelly Rust Remover. This will remove the rust. Also for the handles, you can purchase a product called Linseed Oil. This will preserve the handles on your tools.

Note: I have no financial or commercial interest in any Web sites, products, services, or professionals mentioned in this book.

Silk Plants

I have silk flower arrangements everywhere, and they are dust collectors.

- So when I am cleaning them, if I don't think they are dirty enough to wash, I use my hair dryer on them. This will knock off all or most of the dust that has collected on them.
- You can also purchase a silk cleaner in a spray form, from your local craft store. You can spray it on your silk plants.
- After they get so dirty, I take them apart, wash them in the sink or bathtub, and let them air-dry.

Another great way is an air compressor. Take your silk plants outside. Start slowly making sure that the silk arrangement can withstand the pressure. Note: When they start fading, it's time to toss them and get new ones!

Silver

Silver tarnishes so easily. After you clean and shine your silver pieces, wrap them in a silver cloth. Never store silver in wool. Wool can cause tarnish, which causes corrosion of the metal.

Simple Green Cleaner

Simple green all-purpose cleaner can be found in the automotive section. It is a cleaner that works on a number of things. It works well on food stains, water stains, and carpet stains. It is a good product to have on hand, because it can be used on so many different things. Always test a small area first.

Note: I have no financial or commercial interest in any Web sites, products, services, or professionals mentioned in this book.

Soap Dispensers

Find a pretty dispenser with a pump to put dish washing liquid in. You can also do this with your shampoo, conditioner, and hand soaps. You can purchase these dispensers in many styles and colors.

Statements

Get a three ring binder for your 401(k) statements. Punch holes in them and file by date. File the statements on top each time. When you open your binder, you will always be looking at the latest statement. If you have several accounts, use a big three ring binder. Use dividers to separate them by account, or have individual binders by accounts. Also keep information in the binder that says who the beneficiary is and contact information on the accounts. Keep your binder in a safe place and away from wondering eyes

Stickers

Goo gone spray gel is good for removing sticky residue. Spray it on. Let it set for a few minutes and wipe off. It smells good and is used for many different things.

Note: I have no financial or commercial interest in any Web sites, products, services, or professionals mentioned in this book.

Storing Small Electrical Appliances

Small appliances such as crock pots, melting pots, grills, griddles, electric skillets, juicers, food processors, and toasters are appliances that you wouldn't normally use everyday. Keep them stored in a cabinet or a pantry. This will give you extra counter space.

Storing Christmas Decorations

Christmas trees and Christmas decorations are very expensive. I have been using my decorations for years. I keep adding to them each year. They still look like new. Clear Rubbermaid totes and the under the bed storage containers are a must. They also make boxes just for Christmas decorations. If you use boxes or containers, make sure that they are durable and stackable. I use the under the bed storage containers. They are perfect for the new and used wrapping paper. Take an old pair of panty hose. Cut the legs of each one, then cut the feet off. Slip the leg over the roll of Christmas paper. This will keep it from unrolling. I keep all my decorations separate. I keep my bows, ribbons, nametags, and tapes in one container. My special ornaments in one container, my Christmas balls in one box. I like to find the boxes for my Christmas balls that have the dividers so they won't get broken or damaged. I wrap my lights around a newspaper. I also keep them separate. For beaded garlands, I put each strand in the small Ziploc baggies. This keeps them from getting tangled together.

Once I get everything segregated, I number each box or container. When I get ready to decorate the next time, I know that box numbered #1 goes on the tree first. Once everything has been packed up and numbered, I pack everything into one big box. So when I get ready to decorate for the holidays, I don't have to make so many trips. Note: I do the same with all of the other holiday decorations. Take a picture of your Christmas tree before you take it down just in case you can't remember how you had it decorated and for reference.

Storage Room and Tools

How many times have you been looking for a tool and couldn't find it? Get organized! Start with pegboards and hooks. You can have the pegboards cut to size. Most of your hardware stores offer this service free of charge. Hang your pegboard and start hanging your tools. They make hooks for large and small tools. This will free up your floor space. You can see everything because it is hanging. Note: When hanging items, hang like items with like items. If it can be hung, I hang it.

When I finished hanging all of our tools, I had one section for just items that I purchased and forgot about and these items had never been used. Now before I make a purchase, I check the pegboard to see if I already have it first. Section off part of your storage room make a section for lawn and garden, automotive, athletic, sports equipment, and paints. Now you're in control of your storage room and tools.

Sugar

Have you ever started cooking and realized that you were missing an ingredient such as powder sugar? A quick fix is if you have a coffee grinder, use it to make powder sugar.

Suitcases

If you travel a lot this is not recommended, but if you only travel once in a while, then this is a good tip. When you're not using your suitcases, use them to store off-season clothes.

Sweaters

I never hang my sweaters. I like to fold them. They stay in shape much better. If you don't have a big closet, you could put them in the top of your closet, or if you have a chest of drawers you could store all of them in there. If you don't like that idea, then use the sweater bags that hold about twelve sweaters, and hang it in your closet. The sweater bag hangs over your closet rod and you can fold your sweaters and put them in there. Some have zippers; some are made open in the front for easy access.

Tabletops

Have glass cut for all pieces of furniture. This protects and preserves the furniture. It is very easy to clean. You could always put pictures or old family photos under the glass for display. Check around for the best price.

To-do List

Write down everything you do in a day's time, whatever it is. If it's cleaning a drawer out, running an errand such as going to the bank, the cleaners, whatever it is better write it down. You would be surprised at what you can accomplish in a day even though you feel like you haven't been productive. The list will tell the tale.

To Pit Cherries

A good way to pit cherries is to use the insert from a percolator. Take the long stem from within the percolator, insert it into the top of the cherry and push it through, and now your cherry is pitted.

Tools

Keep a small amount of tools in hand as you never know when you may need them. Keep in a kitchen drawer tools like a hammer, a pouch that holds the different size screwdrivers, a tape measure, and assorted nails/screws. This will keep you from running back and forth to the storage room.

Toothbrush Holder

Use a toothbrush holder for a flower vase. Fill the toothbrush holder with water, and tuck one or two stems into each hole. You'll achieve perfect balance. You could have them all alike, or mix them up with different colors and styles. This is especially good to use if you have a small plant that you are trying to get a root started on.

Towels

Install a wine bottle rack or a metal rack on a wall close to the bathtub. The wine bottle racks hold about six towels. Roll each towel and fit each rolled up towel into that space. Find a decorative basket and place it on the ledge of the bathtub. Roll each washcloth just as you had rolled the towels and place them in the basket. Now you have your towels and washcloths close by.

Trash Cans

To eliminate time and space, keep your trash liners at the bottom of the trash cans. When trash has been removed from the trash can, the liners to the trash can are right there ready to be put on the can.

Transporting Food

To move your dish without spilling it everywhere, place the dish on a shelve liner. This will help in keeping it from shifting. Home Accent Grip-it is a good one. It has a rubbery texture. Also anything that you don't want rolling around on your floorboard or trunk, you can place it on the Grip-it. This will help to keep it in place until you get to where you are going. For small dishes with lids, put a rubber band on it or use tape.

Note: I have no financial or commercial interest in any Web sites, products, services, or professionals mentioned in this book.

Travel Bottles

When we go on a vacation, most hotels have the little travel bottles of shampoo, conditioner, and soap. I like to keep them. You will always have a backup if you run out. If you have grandchildren that occasionally stay over, make them a little goody bag. Put a small bar of soap, shampoo, conditioner, and a toothbrush in there. They will love it!

Tuna

I used to hate making tuna salad simply because draining all the water off seemed to be impossible. That was until I found a simple solution. I open up the tuna cans, remove the lid, and throw it away. Get your strainer out. Empty out each can into the strainer. Let it drain for a second or two. Take your spatula and press all the water out, rotating the tuna. Keep rotating until the tuna has a dry texture.

Umbrellas

Keep your umbrellas by the door so the next time you need one, it will be there and you won't have to spend time hunting for one. Use a decorative container or basket to place by the entryway door. Also if you have a water key tool that you use to cut the water off at the main connection, put the water key tool in the container or basket along with your umbrellas so you will always know where it is, in case of an emergency. If you ever find that you don't have a shade tree to get under and you're working outside in the heat of the day, take an umbrella and a long stick. Use some tie straps or tape and strap, or tape the umbrella to the stick and stick it in the ground, and now you have shade. *(Short story)*

The reason I put this tip in here is because this happened to my husband and me. We had an eighty-foot tree cut down in the dead of the summer of 2009. We had to burn the tree. It was so hot and humid and there was no shade tree to get under. I went to the storage building and found my paint roller extension pole, a large umbrella, and some tie straps. I put it all together and we had a shaded place to get under. I stuck it in the ground between our lawn chairs. We still laugh about it. Desperate times calls for desperate measures!

Vacuum Fix

The next time your vacuum cleaner has something stubborn such as a piece of string, or hair, stuck in its roller bar, remove the offending object with a seam ripper, which will easily cut through knots and tangles. Be sure to unplug the vacuum cleaner before clearing the obstruction.

Vehicle

Do you ever get embarrassed when someone has to ride with you, but before they can sit down, you have to clear off the seat and make room for them? I got into the habit of always taking the items out of my car that I didn't need each time I would get out of my car—things such as cups, papers, toys, and jackets. I like my car to be clean on the inside and smell fresh. I keep a can of air freshener under the seat of my car and everyday before I get out, I spray a little. This is good for smokers.

Also the next time you get an oil change, purchase a new cabin air filter. Have the attendant show you where it is on your car and once a month, pull it out and spray it with your favorite fragrance. I purchased four small inexpensive rugs and placed them over my mats in my floorboards. This keeps my mats from getting soiled. If there are items you must keep in your car, find a bag that zips and keep these items in there not only will your car look organized these items are out of sight and could reduce the chances of break-ins or theft.

Velcro

Velcro can be used on a lot of things such as hanging lightweight pictures. Put a couple of small strips on the wall and the back of the picture. This will help in keeping the picture straight. I like to keep a roll or two in hand. You never know when it might come in handy.

VHS Tapes

VHS tapes are now a thing of the past. If you have VHS tapes to keep out of a landfill, you can send them to *Alternative Community Training*, a nonprofit Missouri company that provides jobs to people with disabilities. The workers erase the tapes, reselling the ones that are in good shape, and recycling the plastic parts of the rest. Mail the tapes (at the cheaper USPS media mail rate) to *act*, 2200 Burlington, Columbia, MO 65202

Note: I have no financial or commercial interest in any Web sites, products, services, or professionals mentioned in this book.

Vintage Online Finds

If you don't have time to yard sale for that vintage or shabby but chic look, go online! For that elegant French flair, go to www.notooshabby.com.

If you are looking for vintage fabric, go to www.rickrack.com
For fabric's, go to www.revivalfabrics.com

Vintage buttons are collectables. You would be amazed at what people would pay for these items such as hats, gloves, dresses, and buttons. So don't throw it away thinking it's junk.

Note: I have no financial or commercial interest in any Web sites, products, services, or professionals mentioned in this book.

Vents

Most homes are laid out differently. Some have the vents in the ceilings, walls, and floors. If your vents are in the wall, or ceiling, you really don't have to worry about this. If your vents are in the floor, you have to worry about dirt and small objects falling through the vents. Remove all floor vents and place a screen under the vent to catch all the dirt and foreign objects. Also to clean the vents, fantastic spray cleaner works well.

Note: I have no financial or commercial interest in any Web sites, products, services, or professionals mentioned in this book.

Wagons

A wagon is a good thing to keep around the house. You could use it for a number of things. If your child has outgrown his or her wagon, don't get rid of it or let it sit and rust. Put it to use. You could use it to move plants around the yard, or to move your groceries from your car to the inside. You could also use the wagon as a decorative piece in your home such as your kitchen, child's room, or outside on the patio, or porch. If you live in a country style home, you could use the wagon in the restroom and store your towels in it. There are a lot of things you could use a wagon for. Note: If you don't have a wagon, look for one at a yard sale.

Walls

A good way to hang pictures is to begin by laying out your pictures on a big piece of Kraft paper and tracing the shapes with a pencil. Label each one to avoid getting them mixed up. Cut out the shapes and arrange them on the wall with painter's tape. Don't be afraid to add an odd shape. This will give it contrast, especially if you're using all square and rectangular shapes varying in frames, sizes, and colors.

To avoid unnecessary nail holes in your wall, use the Kraft paper shapes you've cut out to arrange the pictures. Mark the spot on the Kraft paper, hammer your nail in the wall, take the Kraft paper down, and hang your picture. Note: Once you've taped the Kraft paper cut outs to the wall, you can see what it will look like before you start hammering nails into the wall. Another way is to turn the picture around backward. Make your mark above the hook and make sure to get it level and straight.

Warranty Papers

Are you always searching for a warranty book or paper on an item that you purchased? Start keeping them all together in one location. Every time you make a purchase, date it, and then file it.

Use the expandable file folder. It has all the different pockets. Also you could use Ziploc baggies. Use a permanent marker to label the outside of the bag. This is good if you have anything extra with the warranty papers, you can add this in with the paperwork. An example would be, when I purchased my air mattress an extra patch came with it I filed it with the paperwork. It's all about keeping everything together.

Water Key

If you have a water key tool that you use to cut the water off at the main connection, put the water key tool in the container or basket along with your umbrellas, so you will always know where it is in case of an emergency.

White-canvas Shoes

White-canvas shoes get dirty so easily. You can purchase more than one pair of them, as they are very inexpensive. They wash up very well but never dry them in the dryer. I let them air-dry inside or outside. So while one pair is air-drying, you still can wear white shoes. Also in winter, you can dry them by placing them upside down over a vent or by placing them upside down on top of the dryer.

Who Do I Call

Keep a list of all the important numbers you may need and keep them posted where you will know where to find them, such as the refrigerator. A good source for finding this information would be to contact your *Area Chamber of Commerce*. If you're a member, you should receive an updated copy every year for government and business listings in your area.

Who Gets What When I'm Gone

Imagine you have personal items that you want to pass on to your loved ones after you're gone. But you don't want your loved ones fussing and fighting over these things. The first thing to do is make a *will* and plan ahead. But a neat twist would be to wrap up the items you want to leave to a specific person such as a family member, or a friend, and put that wrapped gift away maybe in an attic with their name and a note attached to it, and give a little history on the item.

I would hate to know that my collectables were going to end up in a yard sale or an estate sale simply because my loved one thought it was junk. So on the bottom of your collectable, put the value of it with a little history (such as my grandmother's teapot value $150 and the date). (Some of my items are marked, don't even think about it.) I tell my kids that if I have it, it's because it means something to me. I understand that they can't or won't keep everything after I'm gone but I don't want something of value sold for twenty-five cent at a yard sale. If you are worried that this might happen to you, it could. So think ahead.

Windows

If you don't have any window cleaner, plain dish soap and water works just as well. After you have washed the window with a soapy cloth, take a dry cloth and wipe until dry. Now they are clean with no streaks. You can also purchase a product called Invisible Glass. It can be found in the automotive section in most stores.

Note: I have no financial or commercial interest in any Web sites, products, services, or professionals mentioned in this book.

Wicker

If the wicker or cane on your patio furniture is starting to sag, fill a bucket with hot water and apply it to the wicker using a sponge. Let the furniture air-dry. The wicker will tighten and shrink back to its normal size.

Wiper Blades

Imagine you live in an area where you get a lot of snow. To make your morning's a little bit easier, cover your wiper blades with a pair of socks each night. This will keep the blades from freezing. Also use an old blanket to cover the windshield. Use one on the front and one on the back glass. Remove and shake off the snow. Lay on a plastic bag in the trunk of your car.

Wire Storage Baskets

Install wire shelving in your pantry or cupboard's. This makes items easier to see. For small bathrooms that don't have a lot of cabinetry, use the sliding wire baskets under the bathroom sink.

Work Clothes

Go to a thrift store or goodwill and purchase your work clothes. I found that wearing oversized pants when I am weed-eating helps in keeping me cooler. I wear a thin pair of shorts under my oversized jeans, when I'm finished I pull the jeans off before I go inside. This keeps me from tracking in grass. Always wear protective eyewear and boots when weed-eating. I tuck my pants legs inside my boots.

Note: I have no financial or commercial interest in any Web sites, products, services, or professionals mentioned in this book.

Yard Clutter

The first impression starts with the appearance of the outside of your home. If you have clutter and junk everywhere, and you don't know where to start, the first thing to do is to decide what is good and what is trash. Get rid of anything you're not using. Store anything you're keeping out of sight. Any tools and lawn equipment should be stored out of the weather. Cut the grass, weed eat and clean out the flowerbeds.

Yard Sales

I used to be so shy about yard sales but my brother, James, and my sister, Cathy, showed me how it was done. They are the yard sale king and queen. Read and learn!

You want to have a yard sale and you want it to be a big hit. But most of all, you want to get rid of some of the clutter and put a little money in your pocket. Have someone helping you. Husband or best friend, etc., make it fun!

• Plan ahead, save your newspaper and bags for the big sale.

- Set a date and run your ad in the local paper. Make sure your signs are posted the night before. Please remove your signs after your sale.
- Purchase your stickers or use painters tape. Price everything. Be organized. Group like-items together such as house ware, sports gear, tools, toys, books, CDs, etc.
- Clean everything and have something for everyone. Make ice tea or lemonade for **the thirsty shoppers** especially if it is hot outside. Set things so it is eye-catching, and makes them want to stop.
- As a general rule, sell bigger items, such as appliances and toys at a third to half of what it would cost now. However that doesn't work for books, CDs and clothes. Put the clothes in size order as it makes it easy for the shopper.
- There's always some bargaining at a good yard sale. It makes the shopper feel like they're getting a deal when you come down on the price a little. On your valuables it is okay to stick to the price.
- **Top selling yard sale items:**
  1. Antiques, vintage glass, and albums
  2. DVDs and CDs
  3. Children's clothes, baby clothes, and toys.
  4. Decorative household items such as lamps, candlesticks, and appliances.
  5. Sports or soda memorabilia (such as Coke and Pepsi bottles).
  6. Vintage chrome appliances and don't forget Elvis Presley.
  7. Buttons

Ziploc Bags

I should be the spokesperson for Ziploc bags. They are great for sorting items that you want to keep separated.

- If you have loose change that you've been saving, and you don't have the coin wrappers, you can place the coins in the Ziploc bags until you can get the wrappers to roll them.
- When traveling, store items that may leak in the baggies such as shampoos, conditioners, soaps, and makeup.
- Use for sorting small toys, game pieces, and cords.
- Anytime you need to crust graham crackers for a piecrust, put them in a Ziploc bag, and then whip out the rolling pin.

There are so many uses for Ziploc bags other than for just food use. I could go on and on.

Note: I have no financial or commercial interest in any Web sites, products, services, or professionals mentioned in this book.

Checklist

The object is to start from the top and work your way down. This list is very detailed and should be used on occasions when you are giving your home a deep cleaning.

Bedroom Checklist

- Does the ceiling need dusting? Do smoke-detector batteries need to be replaced?
- Do ceiling lights, fixtures, or ceiling fans need cleaning or dusting? Do any lights need to be replaced?
- Do ceiling vents or floor vents need dusting?
- Have you dusted the walls?
- Have you dusted all the pictures?
- Has all of the greenery been dusted or washed?

- Have you wiped off the light switches?
- Are the bedroom windows clean? Do the curtains need to be dusted or laundered?
- Are the window seals clean and dust free?
- Do the window blinds need dusting or washing?
- Have you stripped the bed of its dirty linen's? Did you flip your mattress?
- Have you put clean linen's on the bed?
- Have you vacuumed out from under the bed?
- Have you dusted the head and footboard?
- Are your closets neat and orderly?
- Are your nightstands neat and orderly?
- Are your chest of drawers and dresser drawers neat and orderly?
- Have you dusted or polished all bedroom furniture?
- Have you dusted all decorative items in you bedroom?
- Have you hung all clothes up neatly in the closet?
- Are all shoes put away?
- Is everything off the floor?
- Have you emptied the trash can and have you washed it?
- Have you dusted the television front, back, side's and under the VCR, DVR, and all the components? Do the batteries need to be replaced in your remote controls?
- Have you wiped off the telephone?
- Have you wiped off the baseboards? Have you vacuumed?
- Have you dusted all lamps and shades?
- Have you removed everything from the bedroom that doesn't belong in there?

Great Room, Den, or Living Room Checklist

- Do the ceilings need dusting? Does the ceiling smoke detector need the batteries replaced?

- Do the ceiling lights, fixtures, or ceiling fans need dusting? Do the lights need to be replaced?
- Do the walls need dusting?
- Does the door facing need to be washed?
- Have you cleaned the sliding glass door if you have one?
- Do the light switches need to be cleaned off?
- Do the windows and window seals need to be cleaned?
- Do the blinds, shades, or curtains need to be dusted, washed, or laundered?
- Have you dusted all pictures and decorative pieces on the walls?
- Does the greenery need to be dusted, washed, or replaced?
- Have you removed all furniture from the walls and vacuumed behind all furniture?
- Have you cleaned all ceiling vents, floor vents, and baseboards?
- Have you removed all cushions from furniture and vacuumed?
- Have you polished all the furniture, such as coffee table and end tables?
- Have you dusted all lamps and shades?
- Have you dusted the bookcases?
- Have you cleaned out the fireplace?
- Have you cleaned the doors on the front of the fireplace?
- Have you cleaned the mantle?
- Have you cleaned all of the tools for your fireplace?
- Do you have wood, matches for the fireplace? Is the screen proctor clean?
- Have you dusted the entertainment center and all components such as TV, VCR, DVR, and play stations?
- Have you checked the batteries in all the remote controls?
- Have you removed all items that don't belong in this room?
- Do the carpets need to be cleaned?
- Have you swept, mopped, or vacuumed?
- Have you vacuumed all the area rugs?

Kitchen Checklist

- Do ceilings need to be dusted? Do smoke-detector batteries need to be replaced?
- Do ceiling light fixtures need to be washed?
- Do ceiling or floor vents need to be dusted or washed?
- Is the ceiling fan clean and dust free? Do lights need to be replaced?
- Are the walls, doors, and light switches clean?
- Have you dusted all decorative pictures on the walls?
- Does your greenery need to be washed or replaced?
- Are the windows clean inside and out, and are the window seals clean?
- Do you need to launder the curtains?
- Do you need to dust or wash the blinds?
- Do you need to clean or dust the front, top, and sides of the refrigerator?
- Pull refrigerator out from the wall. Sweep and mop it.
- Clean out the inside of the refrigerator. Is the freezer clean? Don't forget the baking soda.
- Have you cleaned the stove top and the inside of the oven?
- Have you cleaned the microwave oven inside and out?
- Have you wiped off all small kitchen appliances?
- Have you loaded the dirty dishes into the dishwasher and started it to wash? Is the front door of the dishwasher clean?
- Wipe off all countertops. Wipe or wash all decorative items on the countertops, including the spice rack. Have you uncluttered all of the kitchen countertops?
- Wipe off the front of the kitchen cabinet doors.
- Is the inside of the kitchen cabinet neat and orderly, including your pots and pans?
- Is your pantry in order?
- Are your kitchen drawers in order?
- Have you wiped off the table and all the chairs?

- Do you need to launder the place mats and napkins?
- Empty the trash and wash the trash can or replace the compacter bag.
- Have you wiped off the kitchen phone?
- Have you swept, mopped, and wiped all baseboards, wax as needed?
- Have you put out fresh dishtowels, hand towels soap, and paper towels?
- Remove anything that doesn't belong in the kitchen.

Restroom Checklist

- Gather all cleaning supplies.
- Do ceilings need dusting; do smoke-detector batteries need to be replaced?
- Do ceiling light fixtures need to be cleaned; do any lights need to be replaced?
- Does ceiling fan need to be cleaned; does any lights need to be replaced?
- Do the ceiling or floor vents need to be dusted?
- Do the walls need to be washed or dusted?
- Do the walls light switches need to be wiped off?
- Do the pictures on the walls need to be dusted?
- Do the windows need to be cleaned?
- Do the window seals need to be wiped off?
- Do the blinds or shades need to be dusted or washed?
- Do the curtains need to be laundered?
- Have you wipe off all the baseboards?
- Have you cleaned the shower, fixtures and shower doors?
- Do the shower curtains need to be laundered?
- Have you cleaned the bathtub, fixtures and soap dish?
- Have you cleaned the sink, vanity and fixtures?
- Have you cleaned the toilet bowl, seat, and lid?

- Have you cleaned the mirrors and all shelves?
- Greenery, does the greenery need to be washed or replaced?
- Have you washed all perfume bottles?
- Have you washed the toothbrush holder, cup, soap dish, and any decorative pieces?
- Laundry closet, is it organized?
- Have you cleaned out all of the drawers are they organized?
- Have you cleaned out from under the vanity; is everything organized and easy to get to?
- Have you cleaned all hairbrushes and combs?
- Have you folded all towels and washcloths neatly
- Are fresh towels out?
- Has fresh soap, shampoo, conditioner, toothpaste, month wash, deodorant been put out? Is it time to change out toothbrushes?
- Tissue in the dispenser.
- Have old magazines been replaced with new ones?
- Sweep, mop, or vacuum.
- Have you emptied the trash can and washed it?
- Do throw rugs need to be laundered?
- Have you removed anything that doesn't belong to the restroom?

Pet Checklist

- Have you checked your pet for fleas?
- Have you treated for fleas?
- Have you changed out his or her flea collar?
- Do you have a collar with your phone number on it in case your pet wonders off, so he or she can be returned to you?
- Has your pet had his or her yearly shots?
- Do you have a file on your pet?
- Has your pet had his or her monthly heart worm medication? Has your pet been groomed? Is it time?

- Have you washed all of your pet's toys, blankets, and sweaters?
- Have you aired out your pet's bed?
- Have you cleaned out the litter box? Wash, air-dry, and fill with new kitty litter.
- Have you given your pet fresh food and water?

Monthly Checklist

By now you should be organized and you should be using the to-be filed file that you made up for all of your monthly bills, which has already been paid for the month. I hope so.

- Balance bank statements.
- Balance savings account statements.
- Pay any bill's that are due.
- From the to-be filed file, file any bills that have been paid for the month.
- Pet's medicine such as fleas, ticks and heart medicine.
- Change air conditioner filter.
- Check to see if any family member's prescriptions need to be refilled.
- Does any family member have a doctor or dentist appointment?
- Do the cars, trucks, or lawnmowers need an oil change?

Yearly Checklist

- Furnace inspection
- Fire extinguishers
- Replace batteries in smoke detectors.
- Replace batteries in carbon monoxide detectors.
- Fireplace
- Gas logs

- Contracts/leases
- Property taxes
- Shots for pets
- Yearly physical examination
- Yearly dental examination
- Yearly eye examination
- Local dues
- Tags for cars
- Inspection for cars
- Insurance for home
- Insurance for cars
- Drivers license renewal
- Income taxes
- State taxes if you work out of state
- College or school tuition
- Burial insurance or policies
- Propane tanks
- Does the sewer system need to be serviced?
- Expired medication's
- Updated medical records
- Updated will/power of attorney
- Update beneficiary information
- Update 401(k), IRAs

Yearly Planner

I keep a yearly planner on my desk, in my handbag, or purse.

I can write down important things in my planner such as due dates, doctor's appointments, meetings, and birthdays. The planner helps me to plan ahead for vacations and upcoming events.

Credits

Jennifer Michelle Photography for the book cover.

Photo by Jennifer Michelle Bennett
www.jennifermichellephotography.com

Please Read

Readers should use this book only as a guide and reference. The information and resources are believed to be a reliable source at the time of this printing.

Note: I have no financial or commercial interest in any Web sites, products, services, or professionals mentioned in this book.

Index

A

abrasive cleaner, using, 79
address labels, 34
aging parents, caring for, 35
air mattress, keeping, 36
antiques, looking for, 36
appliance cleaner, using, 80
attic, cleaning the, 37

B

baby food jars, using, 37
backpacks, making use of, 37
balsamic vinegar, using, 116
bar, stocking the, 38
baskets, using, 40
Bed Rest, 40
bed slats, fixing, 115
beverages, drinking, 41
binders, making, 41
birthday cards, making, 41
blankets, keeping, 42
books, collecting, 42
boots, keeping shape of, 42
bottle cap on nail polish, fixing, 114
business cards, keeping, 44.
    See also cards and letters,
      keeping
buttons, making use of, 45

C

cards and letters, keeping, 45
carpets, taking care of, 45
CD case, designing, 88
CDs, keeping, 46
ceiling fan blades, painting, 46
ceiling fans, cleaning, 46
cell phones, using, 46
ceramic tile cleaner, using, 80
checklist, 145
  bedroom, 145
  monthly, 151
  pet, 150
  yearly, 151
    See also yearly planner,
      keeping a
cherries, pitting, 133
chest of drawers, using, 48
Christmas decorations, storing,
    130
cleaning supplies, keeping, 48
clear containers, using, 48
clogged spray bottles, fixing, 114
closets, sorting items in, 51
clothes
  packing no-longer-worn, 50
  preparing, 49
clothing for emergencies,
    keeping, 49

clutter, cleaning, 51. *See also* yard
    clutter, solving
coats, storing, 52
cold days and nights, warming, 53
colored hangers, assigning, 53
cookbook, making, 52
cooking spray residues, removing,
    117
copper cleaner, using, 80
cords, tagging, 53
cosmetics
  applying, 53
  keeping, 54
crystal, washing, 54
crystal chandelier, cleaning, 54
curling iron, using, 55

D

decorating styles, keeping, 55
decorative storage units, having, 55
determining what to keep and
    what to get rid of, 30
digital picture frame, purchasing,
    56
direct deposit, having, 56
doctors, listing, 57. *See also* list of
    numbers, keeping a
documents, keeping, 57
dog and cat food, storing, 58
dolls or any collectibles,
    purchasing, 48
dresser drawers, using, 58
DVDs, making book of movies
    with, 59

E

earrings, keeping, 59
electrical appliances, storing
    small, 130

emergency grab-and-go file,
    creating, 61
emergency kit
  in car, 62
  for home, 62
  for storm shelter or basement,
    63
entryway, clearing, 59
errands, running, 64

F

fanny packs, using, 65
felt-tip markers, fixing, 114
filing system, setting up, 67
fireplace, using, 67
fireplace odor, diminishing, 67
flea markets, going to, 65
flower vases, washing, 69
food, transporting, 134
food dollar, stretching, 98
frequently called numbers,
    listing, 70
fresh cut flowers, placing, 70
funerals, sending condolences in,
    70

G

gardening tools, painting, 70
gift bags, reusing, 72
gifts
  buying, 71
  for unexpected guests, 71
gift tags, fixing, 72
gift-wrapping papers, storing, 72
girls' night out, having, 73
gloves, making improvised, 104
grease catcher, using, 73
grocery list, making a, 73
grocery receipts, tracking, 74

guest room, preparing, 74

H

handbags, keeping, 75
hats and gloves, keeping, 75
hedges, trimming, 76
heirlooms, labeling, 76
holidays
  preparing for, 77
  shopping for, 78
home movie tapes, labeling, 81
homework, helping with child's,
  81
hosiery, putting, 82
hotlines, posting, 82
house, building new, 43
household chores, doing, 84

I

ice, recycling, 85
ice-cream scoop, using, 85
Internet acronyms, 95
iron skillet, seasoning an, 86

J

jeans or clothes, marking, 86
jewelry
  cleaning, 86
  hanging, 86
junk mail, shredding, 87

K

keepsake items, dedicating, 88
keys, keeping extra, 89
kids' stuff, storing, 88
kitchen cabinet knobs, replacing, 91
kitchen cabinets, organizing, 91

kitchen sink, cleaning, 92
kitty litter, using, 89

L

last will, making a, 141
laundry, doing, 92
laundry room, keeping, 93
leather, drying, 93
less fortunate, giving items to the,
  69
letters and documents,
  preserving, 93
life story, telling, 94
lifestyle change, 29
lightbulbs, regularly replacing, 94
linoleum and vinyl floor cleaner,
  using, 80
list of numbers, keeping a, 140
loose change, keeping, 96
lotion, purchasing, 96

M

magazines, buying, 96
magnets, putting, 97
mails, handling, 97
mascara brush, cleaning, 98
meat, marinating, 99
medical history, collecting, 100
medicines, tracking, 100
memorable items, keeping, 101
message board, making a, 101
muffin pans, using, 102

N

nails, working with, 102
name labels, putting, 102
newspaper clippings, keeping,
  103

O

odors, vanishing, 80
outside shower, installing, 104

P

packing to move, 105
paint, storing leftover, 106
paint colors, using, 106
painting, 106
paint rollers, storing, 107
paint tray, covering, 107
pantry, keeping the, 107
paper cups, using, 108
Party Planning, 108
pencils and pens, fixing, 115
pens, pencils, and markers,
    separating, 111
peroxide, using, 109
pet supplies, keeping, 111
picnic, going on, 37
picnic basket, using, 109
picture frames, personalizing, 110
pictures, separating, 110
pillows, personalizing, 110
place markers, using, 111
place mats, storing, 111
plastic containers, coating, 112
potluck, having, 112
power strip, using, 113
projects, getting too many, 22

Q

quart-size Baggies, using, 115

R

reading glasses, keeping, 117
recipe

all-purpose cleaner and
    deodorizer, 118
cornstarch, 119
cream of tartar, 119
glass cleaner, 117
grease cleaner, 118
heavy-duty scrub, 118
lemon juice, 118
recipe cards, keeping, 116
reflective vest, keeping a, 119
refrigerator, storing items in, 119
ride to school, deciding the, 121
routine, getting into, 30
rugs, fixing, 116
rules to live by, 21

S

salad spinner, getting a, 121
sales rack, going to a, 121
sandpapers, labeling, 122
sandwiches, preparing, 122
scarfs, ties, and belts, placing, 122
scissors, sharpening, 116
scorched pan, fixing, 116
Seasonal Cleaning, 123
seasonal clothes, packing, 123
security system with recorders,
    using, 124
serving pieces, labeling, 116
sewing kit, making a, 124
shampoos, using leftover, 125
sheer panels, washing, 125
sheets, buying, 125
shoe caddies, using, 127
shoes, organizing, 126
shovels, cleaning, 127
silk plants, having, 127
silver, cleaning, 128
simple green cleaner, using, 128
sliding doors, fixing, 114

soap, preserving, 116
soap dispensers, using, 129
stainless steel sink, cleaning, 80
starting point in doing things, 25
statements, filing, 129
stickers, using, 129
sticky iron, fixing, 115
storage room and tools, having, 131
storage spaces, having, 77
sugar, making, 131
suitcases, using, 132
sweaters, keeping, 132

T

tabletops, using, 132
tennis balls, making use of, 43
to-do list, making a, 132
tools, keeping, 133
Tools to Make Life Easier, 24
toothbrush holder, using, 133
towels, keeping, 133
trash cans, using, 134
travel bottles, keeping, 134
tree sap on deck, removing, 115
tuna, making, 135

U

umbrellas, keeping, 135

V

vacuum cleaner, fixing, 136
valuables for insurance, recording, 113

vehicle, cleaning the, 136
Velcro, using, 137
vents, using, 138
VHS tapes, donating, 137
vintage online finds, 137

W

wagons, using, 138
walls, hanging pictures on, 139
warranty papers, keeping, 139
washing off
    bird droppings, 79
    grass stains, 79
    ground-in-dirt, 79
    pollens, 79
water key, placing, 140
weeds, killing, 115
white-canvas shoes, taking care of, 140
wicker, preserving, 142
windows, cleaning, 141
wiper blades, taking care of, 142
wire storage baskets, using, 142
work clothes, purchasing, 142
working together, 24

Y

yard clutter, solving, 143
yard sales, 143
yearly planner, keeping a, 152

Z

Ziploc bags, using, 144